THE HABITAT HOME DECORATOR
BETTER LIGHTING

THE HABITAT HOME DECORATOR

BETTER LIGHTING

JEREMY MYERSON

Consultant: Andre Tammes of the
Lighting Design Partnership, Edinburgh

OCTOPUS CONRAN

Please note. The photographs have been collected
from all over the world to show as varied a range
of ideas as possible within the scope of this
book, so that not all the items featured are
available through Habitat.

First published in 1985 by
Conran Octopus Limited
28-32 Shelton Street
London WC2 9PH

Project editor Liz Wilhide
Art editor Jane Willis
Edited by Judy Martin
Picture research by Keith Bernstein

ISBN 1 85029 026 1

Typeset by SX Composing Ltd.

Printed and bound in Italy

CONTENTS

FIRST PRINCIPLES

Light is central to all our visual experience. It determines shape, reveals colour, and defines texture.

As natural phenomena, sunlight and moonlight are dramatic and inspirational. The revelation of contrast between light and shade on a sunny day, for example, provides a pleasing visual stimulus. By comparison, much modern artificial lighting is a poor imitation of nature: a bland, uniform, patternless, sometimes glaring spread of light that denies us the perception of choice and contrast in our homes when the sun goes down and we switch on the electric lights.

It wasn't always like that: and it need not be like that. Before the availability of domestic electricity flooded large areas indiscriminately with bright light, homes were lit by fires, candles and gas lamps. These pinpoints of light gave a warm glow to dark corners, illuminating areas where people talked, worked and ate. There was a natural intimacy to such lighting arrangements which lighting systems in modern homes have failed to emulate successfully.

Of course, we now have a greater quantity of light at our disposal – and it is relatively inexpensive. But it is not just the quantity that matters – it is the *quality* of light and how we deploy it.

Lighting in interior design

Lighting is the most important element of interior design in the home. It reveals everything else; the furniture, carpets, curtains, *objets d'art*. It is useless to spend a fortune on decorating and furnishing your home if the lighting is going to produce an unrealistic two-dimensional effect.

In the past, the domestic lighting equipment commercially available was considered too crude to simulate properly the soft contrasts of natural sunshine and shadow. But that is no longer true. Today there is a sophisticated technological palette that can match and even surpass the qualities of natural light. You can now mix and paint with artificial light, to create the kind of environment you want.

Modern artificial lighting now has the technological palette to match the warmth and variety of natural light. The night lighting of a house should create an appealing, inviting environment where the subtlety and stimulus of sunlight seems to emanate from inside. The power of light can open up the space or paint each room with a different, individual mood and atmosphere.

The exuberant theatricality of laser light is not ordinarily a feature of domestic lighting schemes, but this fluid, vaporous effect in bold colour shows the potential of lighting's artistic dimension – where the light itself is a distinctive design component.

This interior has an expansive, functional atmosphere under daylight (far right), but at night it is transformed with electric lighting and the natural glow of fire and candles (right). The warm, intimate setting conveys a completely different mood.

An art and a science

Lighting has a functional role in the home to provide a general level of visibility so that we can read, eat, work, watch television and live comfortably. But it also has a broader environmental and aesthetic role, and should be among the first elements you think about when decorating your home. Not only does its dependence on an electrical wiring infrastructure make new installations tiresome and costly if you start to add lighting track, wall sockets or ceiling spotlights to an interior which has already been decorated, but the ability of lighting to transform a room and convey mood should influence all your other furnishing decisions. Furthermore light fittings, known as luminaires, are worthy of investment in their own right as decorative objects.

Too often lighting is an afterthought – forgotten, deliberately ignored, even a source of worry. Many people deny its governing importance in their homes or complain that it is a complex technology too difficult to learn and put into practice. This book explains how you can achieve atmospheric and decorative lighting effects in your home without having to become a fully qualified lighting designer in the process.

Part of the problem has been the peculiar status of lighting as both art and science. The engineering profession regards lighting as an exact, quantifiable science – and it has scared away the general public with its jargon-ridden talk of lumens, wattage, minimum lux levels, angles of distribution, geometric diffusion, and so on. Even architects, who pay careful attention to the points and angles by which natural light will enter

Down to basics

Moving away from that swinging pendant light in the centre of the room – the stock arrangement – is not such a difficult transition as may at first appear, and the transformation of a bright, glaring space into a warm glowing interior is a reward worth pursuing. For all the complicated language that surrounds the subject, lighting design can be reduced to three basic essentials:

- The light source: the quantity and quality of light that the bulb gives out.
- The light fitting: its aesthetic appearance and the way this instrument controls, directs and distributes light.
- The position of the light fitting.

This book is set out to help you explore lighting design in a technical and decorative context. *Designing With Light* looks at the subject in general terms: the light sources, their qualities and properties; and how to create a sense of atmosphere and style with display lighting techniques. *Lighting Area by Area* suggests specific design solutions for individual rooms. Gardens and garages are not forgotten; moving progressively from front gate to back door, there are tips and suggestions on how to make your home more lively and relaxed with lighting. Finally, *Practicalities* turns to the electrics, equipment and accessories needed to achieve these effects.

into the buildings they design, often tamely hand over responsibility for artificial lighting to electrical engineers. These practitioners calculate lighting to nationally agreed mathematical formulae – often with predictably dreary results.

There is another side to lighting: an artistic dimension in which flair, imagination and intuition play a big part. Photographers and theatre-lighting designers have long produced exciting and innovative schemes using improvised methods and an inspirational eye.

Don't let electrical circuitry and scientific jargon stop you exploring the potential of modern domestic lighting. Of course you must aim to master necessary aspects of the technical side of lighting, but a sense of adventure and decorative flair are just as important.

A FRAMEWORK FOR DESIGN

An understanding of the terminology of lighting is an important curtain-raiser to the design process – not least because the terms have become so confused. Not only does the lighting trade call a *lamp* what the public understands to be a *bulb*, but *lighting design* is the expression most commonly used to discuss both the quality of light emanating from the fitting and the product design of the luminaire itself. As a consequence, non-specialists often take more interest in the style of the light fitting than in its performance as a diffuser and distributor of light – and often buy luminaires without having switched them on to see what they look like in action.

To clarify the terms, for the purposes of this book, *lighting design* is, literally, designing in light: the ways light is applied and directed. The design of the instrument which controls the beam is *luminaire design* or *light fittings design*.

Types of lighting

There are four main types of lighting used in the home:

GENERAL LIGHTING Also known as background lighting, this is a direct replacement for natural light and provides a general level of visibility. On its own, it is bland and indiscriminate, but used with other types of lighting, it forms an integral part of an effective lighting scheme.

TASK LIGHTING Well-positioned and well-directed lighting that provides localized light in specific areas for specific tasks. The flexibility of the luminaire and the colour rendering of the light source are particularly important.

ACCENT LIGHTING A key element of creative lighting design, this reveals colour, texture and form by highlighting and painting in the objects around us. Accent lighting can range from a narrow pencil beam to a broad spot.

INFORMATION LIGHTING Also known as orientation or utility lighting, this provides visual information for our safety and comfort. Information lighting is often based in areas of total blackness. The guiding light on the stairwell, a bulkhead by the garage door, and the fluorescent strip above the lift shaft of a block of flats are all examples of information lighting.

Distribution of light

The four different types of lighting – general, task, accent and information – are each achieved by different distributions of light. The distribution depends on the fitting which houses the bulb and which can determine the beam in a wide variety of ways. When choosing a luminaire for your home, consider above all else the way it distributes the light.

There are three major categories of light distribution:

OMNI-DIRECTIONAL A light that disperses in all directions; as from a pendant fitting shaded with a paper globe.

SEMI-DIRECTIONAL The majority of light goes in one direction but a small quantity diffuses in other directions; for example, through the shade of a standard lamp.

DIRECTIONAL All the light travels in one direction, either in a narrow beam (as from a spotlight), or in a broad flood (as in a floodlight), or in a pattern somewhere between the two.

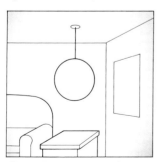

Omni-directional

Semi-directional

Directional

Left: Light distribution can be omni-directional, for general lighting; semi-directional, with light concentrated mainly in one area; or directional, providing a focused beam.

Right: In this open-plan space, mounted fittings supplement light from an uplighter. A downlight links the living area to the kitchen, where spots create efficient task lighting.

Families of light fittings

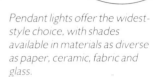

The categories of light distribution can be applied to the twelve families of light fittings found in the home:

PENDANT LIGHTS The most common type of light fitting offering the greatest variety of designs – from paper lanterns to metal cones. The light distributed can be omni-directional, semi-directional or directional, depending on the shade you choose and the length of flex on which the bulb hangs.

Although the pendant fitting provides abundant general light, it tends to flatten shadows and look obtrusive when used as the sole light source. This fitting should be controlled by a dimmer switch, so the light intensity can be altered.

WALL LIGHTS A wall-mounted light fitting that diffuses light into the room, usually through a translucent housing. Again, the light distributed can be omni-directional, semi-directional or directional. Wall lights vary from opaque metal or ceramic bowls, which push most of the light upwards, to glass or perspex cones, which diffuse light gently. Sturdy bulkhead fittings – information lights by the back door, garage or garden steps – are also wall lights.

WALL WASHERS Used to bathe a wall in an even stream of light. Usually ceiling-mounted, recessed into the ceiling or mounted on a lighting track, these lights are wholly directional, using a reflector or baffle to distribute the light at a certain angle, and are very useful for accent lighting.

Pendant lights offer the widest-style choice, with shades available in materials as diverse as paper, ceramic, fabric and glass.

Wall-mounted fittings range from sturdy weatherproof bulkheads giving omni-directional light, to elegant, semi-directional ceramic shields. A more conventional-looking swing-arm lamp allows some adjustment to the lighting's direction.

A pendant light is commonly used as general lighting; the shade over the bulb affects distribution of light.

Wall lights provide discreet accent or background lighting and contribute to the general light level.

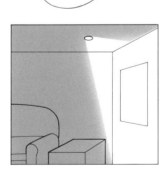

A ceiling-recessed wall washer provides directional light angled to flood down the length of the wall.

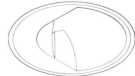

For subtle effects, fully recess wall washers into the ceiling, leaving their silvered reflectors to bathe the wall in a brilliant stream of light.

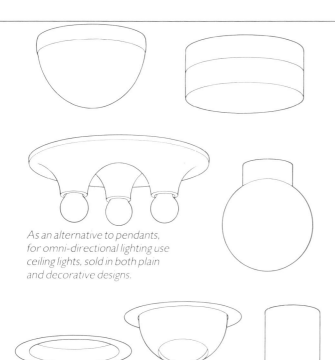

As an alternative to pendants, for omni-directional lighting use ceiling lights, sold in both plain and decorative designs.

CEILING LIGHTS A ceiling-mounted fitting that is not recessed. Usually a globe, it provides a general omni-directional light like the pendant.

DOWNLIGHTS As the name implies, this family provides directional light in a downward stream. A downlight is normally recessed or semi-recessed in to the ceiling, and when fully recessed is one of the most visually inconspicuous and effective luminaires. Depending on the bulb and housing, it can spread light in a narrow, concentrated beam or a broader flood. Eyeball downlights can be swivelled to avoid the tunnel effect rows of rigid downlights can create.

UPLIGHTERS This type of fitting sends semi-directional and directional light upwards. When the beam is bounced off a wall or ceiling, general lighting is achieved indirectly. Free-standing uplighters are important for accent-lighting schemes: position such fittings with care in a room – in a corner or behind a plant – to create interesting effects. Much in vogue nowadays, uplighters have been the subject of considerable design innovation. They can be fitted with a dimmer and some types are switched on with a foot pedal.

SPOTLIGHTS Ceiling-, wall- or floor-mounted, or attached to a lighting track, the spotlight is a flexible, adjustable luminaire that directs light in a controlled beam. It is a most effective tool for accent lighting and the track – developed

Ceiling-mounted downlights can be left prominent or recessed. Swivel 'eyeball' types let you vary the light's direction.

Floor-standing uplighters look like standard lamps, but direct light upwards. Cylindrical versions also provide some light at ground level.

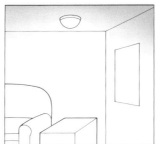

A ceiling-mounted fitting acts as general, omni-directional lighting best supplemented by other sources.

A downlight can be an effective, unobtrusive source of a broad flood or concentrated beam of light.

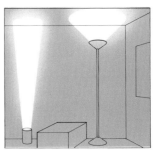

Uplighters can be arranged at different levels, to accent directly or create softened, reflected light.

Available in many designs, spotlights are very versatile. Mount them singly or in groups on powered track. Ready-made clusters can also be purchased.

Table lamps offer a simple way to improve a lighting scheme.

Standard lamps can provide both omni-directional and semi-directional light to create a mood.

initially for commercial use – is a useful accessory for creative design. Essentially, the track is an elongated socket which allows you to attach several luminaires to one electrical source and move them about easily and swiftly. The track can be vertically mounted on a wall, as well as horizontally across a ceiling, for added versatility and different effects.

STANDARD LAMPS Decorative light fittings that are free-standing, usually on the floor, standard lamps distribute omni-directional and semi-directional light, depending on the lampshade. They are best used with a dimmer.

TABLE LAMPS A variety of decorative lights which give a soft omni-directional glow. Very popular for both general and accent lighting, table lamps can be used as bedside reading lights as well as for stylistic effect in the living room.

DESK LIGHTS Essential to provide task lighting, the desk light gives a concentrated directional light over a specific area. The best type of desk light has an adjustable arm so you can direct the light exactly where you want it. Again, desk lights have been the focus of much design innovation and their talents are wasted if used only in study or business areas. A desk light is valuable in the kitchen and makes a versatile bedside light.

STRIP LIGHTING Exactly what the name suggests, strip lights distribute omni-directional and semi-directional light and are useful for all kinds of lighting – general, accent, task and information. Most strip lighting is fluorescent (although

Spotlights are versatile, allowing concentrated beams of light to rise or fall from different angles.

A freestanding standard lamp is a useful supplement to other forms of lighting in the room.

Table lamps provide accent and focus, useful for their decorative effect as well as their function.

tungsten and neon strips can be found in the home). When planning concealed lighting (inside wardrobes, behind bookcases), strip lighting is the most common solution.

VISUAL ODDITIES This heading covers those lights which don't fit into the other eleven categories of luminaire. Usually designed for visual impact rather than the way they distribute light, they provide aesthetic stimulation and amusement. Geese, crescent moons, fabric bag lights, wall-mounted wrapped sweets, giant numbers, and ludicrously large bulbs are just some of the oddities you can buy.

The best lighting design schemes include at least three or four of the twelve families of fittings described here. Deploy them in unusual combinations to banish blandness and develop creative patterns of light.

Frequently, the level of light needed for day-to-day functions is overestimated. Less intense, more subtle and indirect arrangements using three or four light sources in a room will often achieve the same functional level of light while creating a more intimate setting. But, just as knowledge of the existence of paint and brushes won't guarantee a work of art, so the awareness of different luminaires and types of light won't instantly bathe your home in a pleasing glow. As the lighting design professionals will tell you, first you need to examine exactly what you want to achieve.

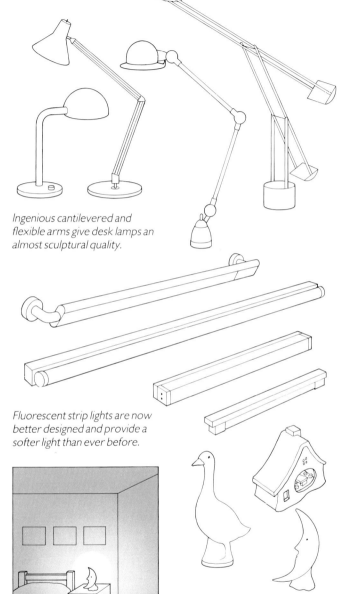

Ingenious cantilevered and flexible arms give desk lamps an almost sculptural quality.

Fluorescent strip lights are now better designed and provide a softer light than ever before.

Providing amusing talking points and unexpected lighting effects, 'novelty' lamps come in all shapes and sizes.

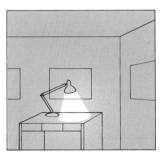

A desk light is a highly efficient form of task lighting, giving a high level of light on a specific area.

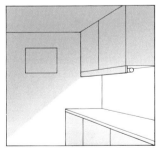

Strip lights perform a variety of functions, with pleasing effect when the source is concealed.

Attractive and eccentric designs for luminaires offer local lighting with a touch of humour.

DESIGNING WITH LIGHT

The real skill of lighting design is to maintain a judicious balance between the practical requirements of illumination and a desire for pleasing or dramatic visual effects. To achieve this, lighting design consultants do considerable groundwork before they even think of specifying luminaires. Careful assessment and analysis of both the home and its occupants is carried out prior to starting the design process.

Invariably, they ask a lot of questions. Which activities take place in which rooms? What plans have already been made for furniture and decor? How old are the occupants? (This is very important, as a sixty-year-old person needs on average fifteen times more light than a child of ten for reading.) How far advanced are the building and decoration of the house? How long do you intend to live in the house? Is energy economy a major factor in how much you are willing to spend? (Lighting is still relatively inexpensive in comparison with other items of home decor expenditure.) What details of your lifestyle will influence the lighting – for example, do you paint or play a musical instrument? How much disruption are you willing to endure during installation? At what times of the day do you use certain rooms? Where are the main entry points of natural light in your home?

Lighting designers have a clear order of priority:

- *Desirability:* for example, do I want to light that surface or object?
- *Practicality:* what equipment do I need? Where shall I position it?
- *Feasibility:* will it work visually in practice? Will it break the budget? Will I be able to change the bulb?

Above all, lighting designers look for opportunities to apply light in a surprising way. If you own, for example, oil paintings, Art Deco pottery or a handsome fireplace, accent them with light to create defined centres of focus. In short, designers look first at what is desirable in terms of effect and then set about trying to achieve it. Functional electrical engineers, in marked contrast, have traditionally looked first at what is feasible and then set about achieving that.

To make the most of your home with lighting, always give desirability a high priority. You can scale down your ambition later, if costs soar or installation proves too tricky. But at the outset, don't be cowed into a cautious provision of light. Look at the full range of equipment available and aim for stimulating, satisfying results.

Lighting is a potent decorative element in the home. This unadorned interior (above) is redesigned with light which creates a sculptural shadow play and vital patterning.

Look for opportunities to apply light in surprising and pleasing ways. A wall light supplemented with candles and an open fire (right) creates an intimate point of focus.

THE RIGHT ATMOSPHERE

Light has a unique ability to convey atmosphere and influence emotion. From shooting stars, lightning and volcanoes to camp fires, fairy lights and fireworks, its dramatic qualities have been a constant source of wonder since time began.

In the same way, modern artificial lighting can do much to influence the mood of an interior and create a sense of drama. Ideally, artificial light should be decoratively pleasing, energy efficient, cost effective to install, and conducive to a healthy environment. The most important factor in achieving these aims is the light source rather than the luminaire.

It is crucial, therefore, to differentiate between the various light sources used domestically, and to understand their individual properties. In choosing a light bulb, three major factors must be considered:

- *Energy efficiency:* how economically the source converts electricity into visible light.
- *Life:* how long the bulb will last.
- *Colour:* how the light reveals colours to the eye, known as colour rendering, and how the bulb itself looks in terms of whiteness, known as colour temperature. (Note that the candle flame, a light source unequalled by modern engineering, has a low colour temperature.)

Light sources

There are three major types of light source for residential use – tungsten, tungsten halogen, and fluorescent – and three less frequently used sources – metal halide, high pressure sodium, and neon – also worth consideration.

Tungsten
The tungsten filament bulb, also known as the incandescent or GLS (General Lighting Service) bulb, has been in service over one hundred years and is still the most popular source of general light in the home. The filament glows white hot and radiates light through a pearlized or clear glass surround, eventually blackening the bulb and burning out. Tungsten has excellent colour rendering with a continuous colour spectrum close to natural light. A low colour temperature gives a warm colour appearance well-suited to domestic environments.

Tungsten's advantages include the fidelity of its colour rendering, warm colour appearance, capacity for dimming, and the fact that it runs off the ordinary domestic mains supply of electricity. The disadvantages are short life and poor energy conversion; it is the least efficient energy converter of all the sources. Also, it generates a fair amount of heat and cannot be used too close to paper, fabric or plastic shades.

Tungsten halogen (mains voltage)
In mains-voltage tungsten halogen bulbs, evaporated matter from the tungsten filament does not blacken the bulb but interacts with halogen gas and redeposits itself on the filament, which glows through a quartz surround. Thus the life of the tungsten halogen bulb is twice that of tungsten, it is marginally more energy efficient, and it matches tungsten's colour rendering; but the colour temperature is higher, giving a less warm colour appearance. It requires no additional electrical control gear and can be dimmed. Its sharp colour appearance makes it particularly useful in spotlights.

Tungsten halogen (low voltage)
The low-voltage tungsten halogen bulb is tiny and compact, making it an excellent and efficient source for discreet accent and display lighting. The colour rendering and appearance are the same as in mains-voltage tungsten halogen, and the low-voltage bulb has greater energy efficiency. It is equipped with a dichroic multi-mirror reflector and can be dimmed – but the major drawback is that it needs a transformer to convert the electric current from mains voltage to low voltage (6, 12, 24 volt).

Fluorescent
Since the late 1930s the fluorescent has been a big rival to the tungsten filament bulb for domestic lighting. It radiates light in a different way, using a gas discharge process in which electrons pass down the inside of the tube and interact with a

Daylight

Tungsten

Tungsten halogen

Fluorescent

The same view seen under different light sources shows how each has its characteristic effect. Daylight is the natural standard, showing up true colours and cleanly defined shapes. But the aim of artificial lighting is not necessarily to reproduce an exact daylight effect. Tungsten and tungsten halogen provide good colour rendering and rich tonal contrast, in which the depth of shadow and brilliance of highlights emphasize form, structure and surface texture. Tungsten halogen has the cooler appearance and casts a slightly crisper light. By contrast, even a warm fluorescent source spreads a flat, even light: shadowing is less emphatic and colours are dulled. It is a functional source within limits, but uninviting and lacking variety.

phosphor coating to enable it to produce the fluorescent glow. Unlike the tungsten bulb which has been virtually unchanged for a century, the fluorescent tube has been continually developed so that now you can dim it – but this is a technically complicated and expensive process.

Fluorescents are long lasting and energy efficient. The cool colour appearance that once made them look alien and unsympathetic in the home (apart from in the kitchen or garage, perhaps) has been modified by the introduction of 'warm' ranges, but the colour rendering is poor compared with tungsten sources.

Mini-fluorescent

Mini-fluorescents come in a variety of shapes, depending on the manufacturer, and can be used in desk lights, task lights, uplighters, wall lights. They are versatile, enjoy a long life, and burn economically. They emit little heat so can be placed close to paper or thin fabric shades.

The disadvantages are that the colour-rendering qualities are not perfect and the colour appearance is intermediate, providing a flat, white, even light not to everyone's taste. The warmer tones of the larger fluorescent strips have not been developed in the mini-fluorescent sector.

Light sources

Light source	Energy efficiency	Average life	Colour rendering	Colour appearance
Tungsten	Poor	1,000 hours	Good	Warm
Tungsten halogen (mains voltage)	Poor	2,000 hours	Good	White, crisp
Tungsten halogen (low voltage)	Fair	2,000 hours	Good	White, crisp
Fluorescent	Good	6,000 hours	Variable	Cool or warm
Mini-fluorescent (energy saving)	Good	5,000 hours	Variable	Intermediate
Metal halide	Very good	6,000 hours	Variable	Cool, white
High pressure sodium	Very good	12,000 hours	Variable	Warm, orangey
Neon	Fair	25,000 hours	Variable	Wide colour range

Metal halide

Metal halide was developed initially for industrial use. Like the fluorescent, it's a gas-discharge lamp which is energy efficient and has a long life but it is neither suitable for home lighting, nor readily available. Its one sensible use in a domestic context is in the garden, where it tends to bring up the natural tones of green very well.

High pressure sodium

Used extensively for street lighting, the high pressure sodium light is the darling of electrical engineers because of its very long life and superb energy efficiency. Lighting designers treat it with less enthusiasm because it washes out colours and turns green to muddy grey. High pressure sodium should be used only where cost effectiveness is critical and colour rendering a good deal less so.

Neon (cold cathode)

Neon, also known as cold cathode, is typically used only for decorative purposes, although some designs for task lights have incorporated neon strip. You can take your pick of colours from lime green to lurid pink. Colour is direct and controllable, depending on the chemical mix of the phosphors in the tube, and the colour of the glass tube itself. The kitsch showboat effect, much admired by graphic designers and advertising agency art directors, can look entertaining and stylish. White neon, running along the top of decorative plaster moulding around a room, is good for architectural delineation.

Once installed, neon lights go on practically for ever, so put them in those awkward places where it is particularly difficult to change a bulb. But beware: neon operates at high voltage so installation should be given over to a specialist.

Exploring the potential

The relationship described earlier between light sources and families of light fittings provides an extraordinary set of visual and technical possibilities. While there are no set rules and improvisation must play an important part in creating the right atmosphere, some guidelines are useful.

Vary positions Bright, evenly lit rooms with no shadow quickly become monotonous and stressful. Aim to inject ambiguity into the spatial arrangements through the lighting, by varying the positions and altering the intensity of the light.

Exploit texture Without shadow no texture is revealed, and the overall impression is two-dimensional and uninter-esting. Shadows are only produced when the light is direc-tional. Therefore, the angle of the light is crucial. If you graze brickwork with light from an angle – for example, with a wall washer – you will be able to reveal the inherent quality of its texture. If you light it straight on with a flat, even light, it will look like a dull brick wall.

Use dimmers Light sources that are dimmable are important in creating variable moods within a space. Dimmer switches provide a relatively inexpensive and uncomplicated way to vary the intensity of light, to suit varying needs at different times of the day and night.

The angle of lighting is crucial to its ability to produce unusual and interesting effects. The rough-cast texture of this interior is exploited under a ceiling-mounted downlight which splashes the wall with obliquely angled light. The effect is dramatic and stimulating.

Orchestrating the environment

Often rooms must perform more than one role. You may, for example, use the living room table for both business conferences and intimate entertaining. So you must design the lighting to create two distinct types of atmosphere: a sense of efficiency and a sense of intimacy.

To achieve a businesslike environment, buy a good quality fluorescent strip unit with deep louvres and mount it across the ceiling to provide crisp, white, general lighting. Use an adjustable-arm desk light to create local task lighting for paperwork and reading.

To orchestrate a sense of intimacy, switch off the fluorescent strip and turn the desk light to face a wall, so that it bounces soft, indirect light off the surface. Switch on glass bowl wall lights with dimmable tungsten bulbs. In addition, arrange a couple of table lights to provide warm points of focus, and position an uplighter in one corner of the room to give a general, reflected glow. Put all these lights on dimmers.

Generally speaking, fluorescents create a crisp, cool interior, while tungsten and tungsten halogen provide a warmer environment. But other factors will influence matters, not least the colour of the walls and the furnishings chosen for a particular room.

No amount of tungsten light will create a warm interior in a space with walls painted icy blue. Therefore the style of your lighting must dovetail with other interior design decisions: you should think about tungsten and fluorescent and neon, and about uplighters and table lights and pendants, at the same time as you plan carpets, curtains and paint finishes.

Orchestrate lighting in relation to the interior design of a room to create a series of different moods. Simply switching off wall lights and turning on a free-standing uplighter (top right) totally alters the original atmosphere (right). And, during daytime, natural light alters the character of the room once again (bottom right).

A MATTER OF STYLE

Interior style is all about personal taste. But whatever your ambitions, the lighting should respond sympathetically to the decor and furnishings you have chosen, at the same time respecting and enhancing the architectural intention of each room. To make sure this integration occurs, decide at the outset what you want to achieve with the decoration of a given space. Then, parallel with other furnishing decisions, look closely at both the visual effects of the light source and at the aesthetic style of the luminaire.

Living with light sources

The wrong type of light cast on a room from the wrong angle can make expensive silk drapes look like cheap fabric and real wood look like imitation laminate. So always experiment with the light source before committing yourself to a rigid and permanent installation.

If you want a really warm, cosy interior, and plan to use, say, a combination of tungsten halogen uplighters, tungsten wall lights and table lamps, don't spoil the effect by purchasing a glacier green carpet or painting the walls charcoal grey. Cheerful and complementary decor partners for tungsten and tungsten halogen are natural timbers, carpets in the orange to brown colour spectrum, and walls painted in 'warm' white and pastel tints. But as both these sources have good colour rendering, they will bring out the best of any colour scheme or combination.

If you genuinely want a cool-looking interior, brilliant white walls have a monochromatic quality that responds to a coolly restrained lighting scheme. But with living space at a premium nowadays, most people want their rooms to perform a variety of tasks – and will aim to achieve a number of different moods. If you are planning to use both tungsten and fluorescent in an interior to vary the setting for business and pleasure, paint the walls pale peach or pale grey. Fluorescent comes up cool, brisk and businesslike; tungsten creates a really warm, glowing environment. The room can be completely transformed at the flick of a switch.

Always try to position luminaires so that the light source itself is not visible within the fitting. There is nothing more disconcerting and stressful than to be constantly reminded of where the light is coming from. Wherever possible, position the light source to shine on objects and surfaces which will cast the light indirectly.

Living with luminaires

Considerable debate rages over the merit and value of various light fittings – and the sort of decorative role they should play. There are two schools of thought on the subject. In one camp are those who believe the luminaire is a discreet, functional tool that should direct and distribute light as

Achieving the most comfortable and attractive interior style is all about coordinating the lighting with the style of the room as a whole. This superbly lit interior (far left) has a simple, easy elegance in which the luminaires are unobtrusive and light sources well concealed. There are discreet points of visual focus in the sculpture accent-lit from below and the wall-hanging lit by a ceiling spot.

unobtrusively as possible. In the other camp are those convinced that the luminaire is a decorative object in its own right, a modern piece of industrial sculpture that should attract visual interest even when switched off. Italian designers, in particular, have been successful in promoting the second viewpoint.

Most lighting design professionals will put the highest priority on a luminaire's functional attributes but there can be no escaping the fact that stylistic appropriateness is extremely important. There is something discouraging about a modern lighting track with heavy black spotlights prominently dis-

Light fittings should be chosen to reflect personal taste and style. The period lamps (top) can be seen as an extension of the art collection on the wall. A classic table lamp design (above) is pleasing and versatile, especially suitable for a country-style setting. Appropriate to traditional furnishings, a tall, arching desk lamp (above right) is as efficient as it is elegant.

The Tizio light (right) is a modern masterpiece of design which has elevated the humble light fitting to the status of a collector's item.

This contemporary hi-tech environment (far right) makes a virtue of solid-looking luminaires entirely appropriate to the leather and chrome furnishings. The focus on a piece of sculpture, lit from above, makes a dramatic accent.

Classic wall-mounted uplighters in metal, glass or ceramic (below) are appropriate for modern or traditional decor.

played in a pastel-shaded, Georgian-style drawing room with ornate plasterwork – or a frilled and lace-fringed pendant shade dangling in a white-walled, modernist interior.

In a sense, the installation of modern, effective lighting technology in a classical, traditional interior poses more problems than designing for a hi-tech environment. It is true to say that the most progressive innovations in lighting technology have emerged in the commercial sector. Uplighters and spotlights, for example, were commonly found in offices, shops and art galleries long before they found their way into domestic use.

Those modern homes that most closely approximate to the visual style of office interiors or shops – rooms with tubular steel display units rather than a Chippendale side-board, plastic floor tiles instead of lush pile carpet, and monochrome blinds in preference to chintz-patterned curtains – will most easily accommodate such elements as lighting track or stark-stemmed uplighters. Furthermore, owners of such homes have the full range of commercial lighting equipment to choose from – not just those items in which the product design has been refined and adapted for conventional domestic use.

For many people, however, such an environment is unremittingly austere and hard to live with for any length of time. They plan their decor to create a softer, more homely effect. It is in this type of setting that the lighting designer must use ingenuity to integrate modern lighting techniques with traditional interior design.

One technique is to recess downlights into the ceiling, to provide lighting from a completely invisible fitting. Another approach is camouflage. If you have attractive oak beams, mini-spots in brown casing can be attached to spread accent light unobtrusively (but remember to clip the wiring to the beam and ensure it is the same colour).

In the same way, harmonious interior design will result when table and standard lamp shades are in colours and fabrics complementary to those of the curtains, cushion covers and tablecloth. If you have a chrome and glass table as a focal point, chrome and glass wall fittings will make a fine match, but be careful not to overdo it.

Remember that you don't have to depend on a central pendant light just because you have a traditional interior. By all means, keep the chandelier, but fit it with a dimmable tungsten bulb set at a low glow, and don't rely on it for general use or task light. Regard it as a decorative object only and supplement it with wall lights and task lights.

Above all, the placing of luminaires in an interior is a matter of intuitive style. Some of the humorous, eye-catching visual oddities available – illuminated skyscraper lights or decorative neon signs, for instance – give a bold flourish to a room and tell people something about you.

Don't be afraid to mix periods. There are a number of classical designs which will look apt and distinguished whatever the decor. If you are a follower of fashion, and your tastes change time and again, light fittings that are truly classical and timeless will prove a worthwhile investment.

A SENSE OF DRAMA

The application of accent lighting is one of the most important and pleasurable elements of creative lighting design. The possessions that adorn our homes – pottery, plants and paintings, for example – are a direct reflection of our lifestyles and the type of people we are. So why not give them a little limelight and make them points of visual focus in a room?

Accent light on an object can be arranged to provide enough reflected illuminance to do away with characterless general light from a central overhead source. The result is a thrilling sense of theatre in your home. Tungsten halogen, which can provide a narrow, pointing finger of concentrated light, is a very useful source in this context. Take a cue from lighting design professionals: scan your home for opportunities to use accent light, and borrow from the lighting repertoire of the theatre, art gallery and shop window.

Even the most unlikely objects add interest to an interior when lit up. Ask yourself the following:
- What should I light?
- What light source and luminaire should I use?
- From what angle should the object be lit?

Again, improvisation is an important part of the design process, but the following are a few tips in relation to particular objects.

Lighting a ceramic object

Any opaque object will reflect light, not transmit it. A large ceramic vase or sculpture can be dramatically lit as the centrepiece of a well-furnished room.

FROM ABOVE Use the narrow beam of a low-voltage tungsten halogen downlight to pick out the upper contours of a ceramic vase. The contrast of light between top and bottom will make it appear to float theatrically in space.

FROM BELOW Floor-mount a tungsten halogen baby spot behind the object. It will appear in virtual silhouette and there will also be a dramatic shadow on the ceiling.

FROM AN ANGLE Use a wall- or ceiling-mounted spotlight or eyeball downlight to beam on to the object from an angle of thirty-five to forty degrees. This will create a more natural, grazing accent light, less dramatically stark.

Lighting a ceramic object

A direct, concentrated beam of light from a downlight above delineates the upper contours of the object while the lower part remains in shade, giving a dramatic effect of tonal contrast.

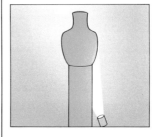

A small spotlight, floor-mounted and casting its beam upwards behind the vase, throws the shape into silhouette, making a mysterious, shadowy form against the background of light.

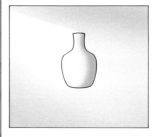

Angled light falling more broadly from one side makes a less theatrical display, but the form is clearly outlined and modelled to show off its natural character. A spotlight or swivelling downlight can be arranged to this effect.

Lighting glassware

The great virtue of glass is its translucence. Exploit its ability to transmit light by lighting glassware from below or behind. Lighting from above ignores its intrinsic qualities.

FROM BELOW If you have glass goblets, place them on a translucent, milky glass shelf. Place a row of low-voltage tungsten halogen spotlights beneath the shelf, or attach a fluorescent strip behind a baffle on the wall. The result is a beautiful 'light box' effect.

FROM BEHIND Use wall-mounted fluorescent strips (tungsten halogen doesn't produce the flat, uniform light needed) to diffuse light gently on to the glassware through a translucent screen of semi-opaque glass, fabric or perspex to achieve an attractive delineation of shape.

Lighting glassware

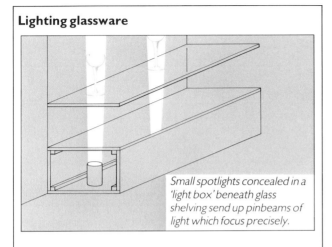

Small spotlights concealed in a 'light box' beneath glass shelving send up pinbeams of light which focus precisely.

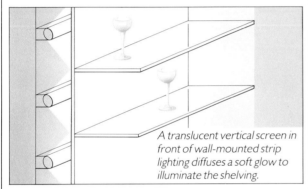

A translucent vertical screen in front of wall-mounted strip lighting diffuses a soft glow to illuminate the shelving.

Lighting books

The texture and typographic interest of rows of books are worth accenting, so use wall washers recessed or semi-recessed into the ceiling, to graze your bookshelves with light from an angle, emphasizing effects of shadow and texture. Alternatively, clip spots to the underside of shelves and skim light along their length. Remember to think about the lighting for your books at the same time as you plan your shelving.

Lighting pictures

We have all seen the inadequate illumination, reflections and glare that result when pictures are lit incorrectly. It is a subtle art which demands care and attention; with oil paintings in particular, it is important to avoid accenting the heavier

Ceiling-recessed eyeball downlights throw soft pools of light on books and a decorative wall-hanging – a means of highlighting your favourite possessions with a flourish.

Lighting pictures

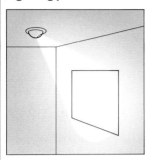

A ceiling-recessed, swivelling eyeball downlight sheds a broad beam over the picture and the area it occupies.

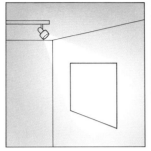

An adjustable spotlight gives a directional spread of light over the appropriate area, tending to centralize the focus.

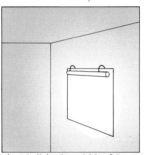

A strip light the width of the painting, mounted on the frame, should cast even light, from top to bottom.

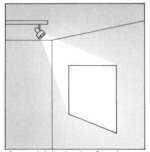

A special device is a framing spot with shutters that lights the picture area exactly, concentrating the attention.

Lighting plants

A broad, angled beam from a spotlight above and behind the plant illuminates its pattern and texture.

An uplighter on the floor bounces soft light off the wall, to create a subtle pattern of light and shade.

texture on the ridges of the brushstrokes – this happens if the angle of the light is too steep. There are four basic options for lighting pictures:

A SWIVELLING EYEBALL DOWNLIGHT, recessed into the ceiling, spreads a broad beam over the painting.

AN ADJUSTABLE SPOTLIGHT on a ceiling track projects a controlled beam on to the painting. Take care to respect the artist's intention in the use of light and shade. (A glance at the Dutch Masters will reveal that they used light in a supremely skilled fashion.) Point the beam at the likeliest focal point of light in the painting.

A SPECIAL PICTURE LIGHT extends over the frame of the painting. You can choose from a range of designs, but try to avoid the imbalance often seen in the picture lighting of stately homes open to the public, whereby the picture is brighter at the top than at the bottom.

A FRAMING SPOT on a ceiling track is a specialist piece of equipment with framing shutters designed to produce a perfect square of light that you can adjust to the size of your picture. This luminaire is accurate but expensive, and therefore best used only if you have a particularly fine or valuable painting and want to make it a special focal point.

Lighting plants

Plants look attractive when revealed by accent lighting, but they also need plenty of light for survival and growth. Place them directly in the line of natural light entering a room, and if there is very limited natural light, shine special plant-

Left: Just as white walls create a more spacious feeling, so a tight or low space is opened out by a wash of light over surfaces. Natural and artificial light give a visual lift to this sloping ceiling.

Below: Dramatic patterns can be created by uplighting a plant from behind. A baby spot on the floor bounces light off the wall, transforming this tall, narrow-stemmed plant.

irridation light sources on to them after dark to ensure they receive enough ultraviolet light.

There are a number of ways to light plants. If the plant pot is in the corner of a room, place an uplighter or floor-mounted baby spot behind it and allow light to bounce off wall and ceiling, diffusing back through the foliage to create imaginative patterns of shadow. Light a plant from above with a downlight to create a pleasant glow, or place a low-voltage tungsten halogen fitting on a spike in the soil for a fairy-light effect. This is especially useful for tumbling plants in baskets.

Avoid placing the light source too close to foliage or the leaves will burn. With spotlights, use a wide angle of directional beam to fall on the whole shape of a large plant; a narrow beam will light no more than a couple of leaves.

Highlighting architectural features

Use the three-dimensional geometry of your room to advantage, exploiting architectural detail with light to create a new visual aspect. Architectural features fall into two main categories: large planar expanses of wall and ceiling, or smaller elements such as column heads, decorative plaster-work, niches and cornices.

Light the large areas with uplighters and wall washers, using light to soften the surfaces of your room. If you have a sloping cottage roof and oak beams, fix spots to the beams pointing upwards, to create a sense of warmth in the cavernous hollow beneath the roof. Treat architectural detail in the same way you would a solid ceramic object: use tungsten halogen spotlights or eyeball downlights to pick out features.

PLAYING VISUAL TRICKS

Theatre-set designers and photographers have long been adept at using light to change our perception of space and structure. You can do the same, improving various aspects of your home with simple lighting arrangements.

Creating space
If you reveal everything with a harsh, bright light and give utterly concise visual information, you automatically define all boundaries and close yourself in psychologically. But if you create a sense of spatial ambiguity with soft, varied points of angled light and resulting patterns of shadow, the room gives an impression of more space and freedom of movement.

Pull sofas and plants away from the walls and put tungsten uplighters behind them, bouncing warm light off walls and ceilings. Just as a room with all surfaces painted white looks more spacious, so you should paint planar surfaces with light, using wall washers and uplighters to give the impression of more space. But don't overdo the ambiguity: there must be sufficient light or the atmosphere will become gloomy and breed insecurity.

Redefining space
When lighting a very large room, avoid omni-directional fittings and don't shine light directly on to the outer walls and ceiling, as this will only accentuate the vastness of the space. Try to create a clearly defined small space within the larger area using localized lighting. Use a combination of wall lights, wall-mounted spotlights, desk lights and table lamps to create visual focus – around a sofa, fireplace, or table, for example.

Don't leave the rest of the room in total blackness; allow some light to diffuse through the space and reflect off different surfaces. If the ceiling is very high, avoid any style of luminaire which sends a narrow shaft of light shooting down into the room from above.

In effect, the development of a localized area with artificial lighting creates quite different impressions of the space between day and night. By day the room is expansive as sun pours in through picture windows. At night a tight ring of light contracts the space to create a more intimate setting.

A large, open space presents the opportunity to play pools of diffused light into different areas of the room. The effect here is powerfully achieved with spotlights in the roof cavity.

A small room seems larger when the furniture is moved away from the walls (top) and the interior is painted with soft light from wall lights or downlights.

In a spacious room pools of light define separate areas (above): note the pendant over the dining table, the downlight or spot to accent a particular point of focus, and the table lamp.

Right: A pleasing sense of visual ambiguity is created on either side of this glass structure by parallel pools of downlight playing on well-positioned plants, picking up their texture.

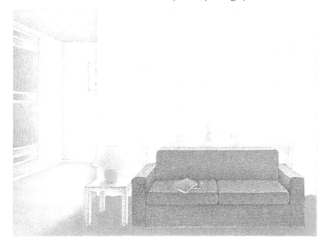

Above: A wall mirror not only makes a space seem larger, but also softens the architectural severity of an end wall, here emphasized by an accent-lit house plant set directly in front of the glass.

Top: Some subtle lighting tricks need the help of props. A thin fabric screen hung across a room appears translucent when lit from behind; lit from the front it becomes a totally opaque room divider.

Playing with mirrors

The potential of the mirror to repeat and extend light without the need for additional energy and equipment has long been exploited by interior designers. The cardinal rule is never to shine light directly into the mirror. Therefore the angle of the light is crucial so that wherever you stand you aren't blinded by the glare.

Two light-reflecting mirrors directly opposite each other will create a feeling of infinite space. If you place a mirror at the end of a passageway and light an object immediately in front of it – a plant, for example – reflected light will create a sense of visual ambiguity which softens the architectural severity of the narrow space blocked by the end wall.

Shadow play and silhouette can be skilfully conjured with mirrors. A favourite trick of the stage-lighting designer – lighting a thin diaphanous gauze from the front to create a solid wall and from behind to create a translucent screen – can be adapted with two-way mirrors used between rooms or in a conservatory. Light them from the front to create an opaque shield; light them from behind so that you can see through into another room.

Dissolving structure

If you have a glass conservatory attached to your home, you can create a pleasing sense of visual ambiguity at night by dissolving the structure with light. Create a single pattern of light in the living room, extend it to the conservatory, and out on to the terrace. The pools of light on either side of the building will dissolve the glass.

Disguising architectural faults

Light can often be unkind in its revelation – even if it is soft and indirect. The only way to hide architectural faults completely is to switch off the light and plunge everything into darkness!

That said, lighting can be controlled to de-emphasize certain points in a room, by focusing on its better aspects. Take everyone's eyes off a damp wall or sloping shelf by accent lighting the rubber plant or strategically positioning table lamps to create soft points of focus.

ENTERTAINING WITH LIGHT

The ability of light to convey a sense of occasion and festivity is an important asset for all kinds of entertaining in the home. Parties provide a golden opportunity to supplement your conventional lighting arrangements with temporary solutions – adventurous, colourful ideas that you may not want to live with all the year round, but which are great fun for an afternoon, evening or a couple of days.

Eating outdoors

The focal point of a barbecue will be the live flame, heat, smoke and food. Take this as your cue and use smoke flares on the lawn and camping-gas lamps behind the bushes to create an atmospheric effect – a warm glow in the distant vista or a close ring of light.

Whatever the occasion small amounts of well-placed light in the blackness of your garden will have an extraordinarily dramatic effect, given the sheer extent of contrast, but take care where you position the sources. If you have an old wall covered with ivy, wash it with light from a spotlight to reveal the interesting texture. If you have a swimming pool or jacuzzi, switch on the underwater lights.

Above all, aim to create silhouettes, shapes and small pockets of visual focus. Uplighting behind bushes adjacent to the eating area is useful to produce moving shadows. But allow enough light to avoid the problem of guests stumbling around in the dark with plates of food. By improvising with light, you will amaze not only your guests, but also your neighbours, who know your garden well by daylight but will see it in a brand new light at night.

Christmas

Christmas lighting should be ethereal rather than overt, to create a sense of wonder in young children and a feeling of intimacy for the whole family. Low-voltage tungsten halogen 'sparkler' fittings are useful to supplement the cosy, warm appeal of strings of fairy and silver lights. Avoid brashly coloured bulbs as they destroy a delicate atmosphere.

One way to make more use of your Christmas decorative lights is to buy a string of fairy-light fittings which are

Special lighting effects can be appropriate and still surprising. Strands of sparkling fairy lights coiled into perspex boxes (above) are a clever new trick with a traditional form. Colourful flares on the lawn (left) are an alluring background to a barbecue outdoors.

The pleasures of eating outdoors are enhanced by magical,
temporary lighting effects. An
array of candles can be relied
upon to add an air of enchant-
ment. Glass containers shield
the flames and contribute their
own sparkle to the occasion.

weatherproof and suitable for outdoor use. You can string them up outside for summer evening parties and bring them indoors to adorn the Christmas tree in winter. To add dramatic impact to your Christmas tree, uplight it from behind with a floor-mounted baby spot or uplighter. Reflected light will create pleasing foliage patterns on the ceiling.

Candles are an essential feature of Christmas lighting. Arrange them in elegant groupings on coloured trays, decorate them with foliage and dried flowers, and they will bring a warm, magical feeling to the festivities.

Children's parties

It is important to keep the lighting bright: a sophisticated, smoochy atmosphere is inappropriate and, anyway, you need to keep an eye on the kids. Candles and flares are dangerous when young children are around and delicate, temporary lighting structures invariably get knocked over.

The safest, jolliest solution is to replace the tungsten bulbs in your ordinary fittings – desk lights, wall lights, pendants – with brightly coloured light sources. Also, to hold the attention of the generation of tiny TV addicts, project cartoons, videos and slides on to walls or screens.

Dinner parties

Candlelight creates a glowing, sympathetic ambience for dinner parties. It brings a warm sparkle to silverware and glassware, it creates a private pool of light and provides a focus for intimate conversation. It also has a cosmetic effect, in that it leaves large areas of the room in discreet shadow, to conceal dirty dishes, serving bowls and so on: this contributes to your image as a natural host or hostess.

If you are worried that candlelight will provide insufficient illumination – for example, when entertaining more than twelve guests – supplement it with dimmable tungsten halogen downlights which create appealing and dramatic shards of light. Switch off all your usual accent lights on plants and books so that the dinner table becomes the uncontested focal point.

A rise-and-fall pendant fitting on a flex is useful for entertaining. If you bring it in low, position candles around the perimeter of the room rather than on the table.

The important point to remember with a pendant is that you must position it exactly, placing the pendant high enough to give unobstructed view to each dinner guest but low enough to conceal the gleaming bulb. With that in mind, it is best to choose a pendant which houses the bulb high up inside the fitting, and put the pendant on a dimmer switch.

Candlelight is a welcome feature of entertaining in the evening; elegant groupings strike the right note (below).

A soft, discreetly positioned lamp (left) is a good supplement to candlelight at dinner.

Disco

Unless you're a technical genius it is best to hire a light show from a specialist firm, but avoid being palmed off with the standard package – a bank of static flashing lights or a couple of stock, clichéd effects.

Disco equipment provides the opportunity to bring all your party rooms alive with light, not just the dancing area. Help out the disco lighting equipment by putting a light under the sofa so that the furniture looks as though it is about to lift off. Strongly accent light your possessions to create all kinds of interesting shadows.

Sound-to-light units will produce flashing lights in time with pulsating music. Strobe lighting causes excitement, but don't overplay it all night long as it can get monotonous and is disturbing to some people. Image projection is another good idea – project videos or slides on to giant screens or white walls to build the party mood. Above all, aim for colour, movement and excitement.

LIGHTING AREA BY AREA

Your home is essentially made up of a number of discrete but interlinked spaces. Although each room should be treated individually in terms of lighting style, with a design solution to suit the tasks performed in the room and the atmosphere you want to achieve, always observe how the different spaces relate to each other in terms of progression and eye adaptation.

When you step into sunlight after an afternoon spent in the darkness of the cinema, it takes a while for your eyes to adapt to the intensity of light and you are momentarily disoriented. If there are extreme contrasts of this kind between different spaces in your home, the effect is unpleasant and can even be dangerous. Don't allow visitors to plunge headlong from a brightly lit living room into a pitch-black hallway, for instance. Think about how your lighting scheme will work as a totality, linking different moods and fuctions.

This doesn't mean, of course, that you should use exactly the same light levels and types of luminaires throughout your home – even if it's a small apartment. That kind of lighting is a recipe for boredom. Different styles of luminaires with equally different ways of distributing light give a small home visual variety and impact. Simply, when you plan your lighting break down your home into a series of smaller interdependent spaces.

Rooms can be split into two categories: those with a single, fixed functional use and multi-functional spaces that require more flexible lighting design with the accent on decorative style and mood. When planning each room, draw a pencil sketch showing the architectural contours, windows and doors, furniture, shelving, decorative objects and plants. Mark also the angles of entry of natural light and the electrical sockets and switches. All such details are important to your planning – poorly positioned or insensitively styled switches can spoil the effect of a room just as easily as an inappropriate choice of luminaires.

Left: A glass façade gives a clear view of the interdependence of interior spaces. A good lighting scheme takes account of visual links between one room and the next.

Below: A hallway should provide an easy transition between the light levels in adjoining rooms. An internal space can need artificial light during the day.

For each individual space, ask yourself the questions examined earlier in the context of looking at your home as a whole, and weigh up the pros and cons of using different types of light sources and fittings.

There is no single, correct way to light a given space; each room can be lit in half-a-dozen different ways and the solution you find the most comfortable and stylish will be very much up to you. However, there are some cardinal rules you should follow in designing with light:

- *General lighting:* avoid glare and tiring, disorienting extremes of contrast;
- *Task lighting:* always put the light exactly where it is needed – on desk or workbench, for example;
- *Accent lighting:* be clear in your intent and direct attention unambiguously towards those objects and surfaces you want to highlight;
- *Information lighting:* make sure you give the right visual information, and in good time – for example, in lighting a concealed back door step.

In all areas, lighting design comes back to the trio of basic choices: the light source, light fitting, and position of the equipment.

MAKING AN ENTRANCE

Entrance information lighting can double as a decorative feature too: accenting brickwork and plant textures while showing up steps and making a warm welcome.

Effective and attractive entrance lighting plays a number of important roles. It provides visual information at night to guide visitors safely through the front gate and up the driveway or path to the front door, where the number, keyhole, and knocker or door bell are clearly illuminated. It gives your home a pleasing or decorative glow from afar which is warm and inviting, and also has a security function in deterring burglars. Especially in the case of a detached or isolated house, floodlights which surround it with a broad spread of white light will deny intruders the cover of darkness.

Gates and driveways

In cities with a high level of street lighting, identifying the house from the road is usually easy enough. But down dark country lanes, cottages are easily passed by unless the front gate is illuminated – ground-recessed uplighters are a good idea for this function.

Once inside the gate, the drive and pathways should be lit up, as a clear guide to the front door for those in cars or on foot. Tough bollard lights which demarcate the driveway provide a good solution – but if you plan a decorative lighting scheme for your garden it can also be designed to double up as entrance information lighting. Uplit trees and rockeries can deflect enough light to show up the path quite distinctly.

Whatever the means you choose to light the driveway, never shine light directly into the eyes of incoming visitors. It is disconcerting and unfriendly, and can be dangerously dazzling to motorists.

Front doors and porches

There is a wide variety of light fittings for front doors and porches, ranging from Victoriana to space-age styling. Choose carefully, bearing in mind the architectural character of your home and the first impression you want to give.

A simple omni-directional fitting distributing warm light is a good decorative solution, but supplement it with directional downlights mounted above the front door, so the keyhole is well lit. One of the common faults of home lighting is a shadowy front doorway half-lit by a side-mounted fitting.

Also, remember to light up the number and .name of your home. There are eye-catching illuminated numerals on the market, but an alternative method is to graze the number with angled light from a wall-mounted tungsten mini-spot.

Entrance lighting is sometimes connected to security time-switches and computer controls; these turn lights on and off at different times to confuse potential burglars. Usually, however, these lights stay on continually throughout the night so, whenever possible, choose light sources that are energy efficient. Mini-fluorescents are excellent for awkwardly positioned porch lights which must work long hours but are difficult to reach to change the bulb. All entrance fittings should be sturdy and waterproof, to resist vandals as well as the weather.

Outdoor lights

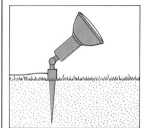

Spiked spotlights with cables above ground can be set in soil where you need them.

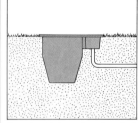

Standard (above) and angled (below) well lights are good at defining garden paths.

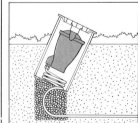

To be safe, outdoor lighting must be very carefully installed and maintained. Check insulation on fittings and cables, and ensure surrounding soil does not become waterlogged.

HALLS, STAIRS AND LANDINGS

This staircase is lit by an unconventional method. Lights in the wall above each step send shafts of light along the treads, forming an ascending pattern of haloes opposite.

Hallways, staircases and landings are transitional areas, between rooms and between the interior and exterior. They have a pivotal role to play in any lghting design, to ensure that eye adaptation to different light levels in different parts of the house is progressive and pleasant. Furthermore, these corridor areas are often difficult to furnish imaginatively, so lighting takes on an added significance as the only really potent decorative element that can be utilized. Too often, though, these spaces are neglected in terms of light.

Hallways
In a narrow hall, low pendant lights will get in the way. Try ceiling-recessed downlights and strategically placed mirrors to give an impression of space, or position tungsten wall lights to give a soft, semi-directional glow. Never direct light into the faces of visitors as they come through the front door. Put all hall fittings on a dimmer so you can vary the intensity of light in response to the quality of light outside.

An imaginative way to light up the hall is to conceal fluorescent lighting behind cornices, or behind a wall-mounted decorative object. A narrow-stemmed uplighter which doubles as a coat stand is another polished combination of function and flair.

Staircases
Safety is an important element in plans for staircase lighting. It is unsatisfactory and potentially dangerous either to leave the staircase in darkness or to wash it with light indiscriminately. In both cases you lose definition of the edges of the steps. The most important aim is to create a shadow which reveals the rise and tread of each step. The simplest way to achieve this is to position a luminaire at the top of the flight of stairs – a ceiling light, pendant or downlight. The angle of the staircase will do the rest. If you choose a pendant, make sure the filament of the bulb is not shining nakedly into the eyes of a person coming up the stairs.

More complicated arrangements include tiny, cinema-style recessed lights or concealed fluorescent strips on each step. People with ultra-modern homes sometimes go to the

expense of installing coloured neon or fluorescent tubes running the length of the bannisters – but this solution is more style-conscious than safety-conscious.

Two-way delay switches between top and bottom of the staircase are a good idea. So, too, is a mini-fluorescent bulb in the fitting at the top of the staircase: its energy efficiency means that you won't need to change it so often in what is usually an inaccessible spot.

Landings
As with hallways, put all landing luminaires on a dimmer. Soft, omni-directional light is best. Children and guests may appreciate a night light to guide them from bedroom to bathroom, so tiny, low-voltage and low-glow fittings at ankle height will be useful here.

Lighting the stairs

Recessed lights at the side of each step show the treads clearly and make an unusual, stylish feature.

A light source at the top of the stairs sculptures every step in a precise pattern of light and shade.

Ceiling-mounted downlights create attractive pools of light on this landing while lighting from an upper level delineates clearly the rise and tread of each step on the staircase. The effect is warm, comfortable and, above all, safe.

LIVING ROOMS

The living room is the focal point of your entire home: the place where you enjoy a communal life with the other members of your family, watch television, work and play. You will probably spend more time in it than in any other room in the house. You may therefore be willing to spend more money on furnishing it and naturally this room has the greatest demands placed on it in terms of lighting.

The sheer diversity of activity that goes on in the living room means that your lighting scheme should combine general, task and accent lighting and be an intelligent synthesis of all the points discussed earlier in the book. Review it not only in terms of general and task lighting suited to your needs, but also with emphasis on atmosphere, style and any special effects you wish to create.

Two views of the same room, from opposite ends, show how the lighting creates different focal points, moods and spatial relationships within the space. Ceiling-mounted spotlights accent-light pictures and books (below) with lamps and candles making soft pools of local light. At the other end of the room (right) the spotlights are used as general lighting, with a single table lamp creating a defined focal point.

Look first at the architectural contours of the room. Is it too small or too big? Can lighting improve this aspect? How do your decor plans relate to the colour qualities of the light sources and style of luminaires? What decorative objects are worth accenting with light? What jobs do you intend to do in your living room that will require special task lighting?

The options open to you are many. But bear in mind one cardinal rule: keep your design flexible.

Keep it flexible

In a living room which must adapt to a series of different emotional moods and physical requirements, it is important to avoid fixed relationships between the lighting and the furniture. You may want to change your mind about how to hang a painting and where to position the sofa. Furthermore, as decor products become more and more like couture clothing, changing with the seasons, you may wish to acquire new furnishing accessories, replace or give a new look to even the major items of furniture.

Portable fittings – table lamps, desklights, standard lamps and freestanding uplighters – are very useful and flexible

design tools, creating intimate rings of light. So too are spotlights that you can reposition at will along a track.

Generally speaking, don't decide on ceiling-recessed downlights unless you are absolutely sure about the long-term uses and style of the room. Make design decisions that are easily reversed – an uplighter standing on a carpet and plugged into a wall socket leaves your options open; a hole cut in the ceiling does not.

Tungsten and tungsten halogen are the best light sources for the living room. Concealed accent lighting behind cornices, bookshelves, and glassware displays make an effective complement to the general level of lighting. Put all lights on dimmers – the variety of moods you will require, and the subtle balances of artificial light with incoming natural light, make this imperative.

As well as creating accent lighting for plants, books and paintings, don't forget to position a useful task light close to the stereo, video rack, computer and record collection. This could be a spot mounted on a short piece of track or clipped to the edge of a book or record shelf, or a wall-mounted adjustable-arm fitting.

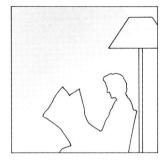

No shadow falls across reading matter if it is lit from above and behind.

A tall uplighter placed behind the television (far left) won't interfere with the screen image. For reading, a broad spread of light from a lamp at one side (left) is efficient and relaxing.

Lighting and decor dovetail in this arrangement of mirror and wall lights.

Watching television

Never watch television without additional lighting. The extreme brightness of the screen in contrast to the darkness of the room will damage your eyes. Equally, avoid positioning luminaires where they cause reflections on the screen, as happens if they are close by the viewer, for example. The best solutions are to place a light behind the television set or deploy light sources elsewhere in the room to bounce indirect general light off walls and other surfaces.

Reading

Focusing on a printed text in a bright pool of light surrounded by complete blackness is very tiring for the eyes. A light source positioned too close to the reader is tiring in itself. Directional fittings such as spotlights are not suited to comfortable, relaxed reading: the best solutions are traditional standard and table lamps positioned beside or some way behind the reader. These luminaires give off a soft, omni-directional glow but will throw enough direct light on to the page for reading. Supplement the general light level with other light sources glowing in the background.

Fitting a dimmer

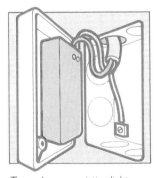 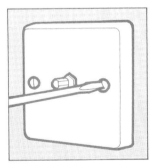

To replace an existing light switch with a dimmer, turn off the power at the mains, undo the screws in the switch's face plate and ease it away from the wall. Disconnect the red and black wires from the switch terminals, and connect them to the dimmer's terminals according to the manufacturer's instructions. Finally, screw the dimmer to the original switch mounting box and restore the power.

DINING ROOMS

A deep shade on the pendant directs a pool of light on the dining table without glare from the bulb. Other sources of light spread a warm ring that reinforces the central focus.

You can be the greatest cook in the world, but if poor lighting in your dining room makes your vegetables look tired and the chicken look synthetic, then your meal is off to a bad start. If you're lucky enough to have a self-contained room reserved solely for the purpose of dining, you have a golden opportunity to create a cosy, dramatic, singular setting which enhances the quality of the food and stimulates relaxed conversation.

You don't need a general level of background lighting in your dining room, unless the table regularly doubles as a work surface. Concentrate all light on to the dining table. The most common fitting performing this function is a rise-and-fall pendant. When you are giving a candlelit dinner, the pendant can be lifted up out of sight. When you bring it in low, remember to position it at a level that does not obstruct the eye contact of your guests but is not so high that it exposes the glare of the bulb. Avoid a harsh quality of strong light from a central source that will cast unflattering shadows. For everyday dining, fix a level that is effective and comfortable for all members of the family.

Experiment to find the right balance. Put the pendant on a dimmer and choose a luminaire which houses the light source high up inside the fitting. The level of light is important: too bright, and the reflections from cutlery and glassware will be painful: too dim, and the diners' faces will recede into the gloom. A good lighting design can be subtle without seeming anonymous; it can add brilliance without being intrusive.

An alternative lighting scheme is eyeball tungsten halogen downlights in the ceiling augmented with candles around the perimeter of the room. Concealed fluorescent strips above the serving hatch and behind a corner cabinet will not detract from the visual focus.

It is important to use tungsten and tungsten halogen sources in the dining room because of the excellence of the colour rendering. If a tomato and avocado salad takes on a uniform muddy tone, it looks unreal and unappetizing. The appearance of food is just as important as the taste, whether the occasion is a quiet family supper or a formal dinner with business associates.

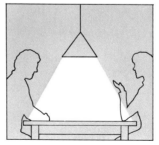

A pendant light should be hung at a level that lights the table clearly without obstructing the line of vision.

A downlight creates an attractive central focus on the table and can be supplemented by other sources.

The cool, uncluttered feel of this dining room is carried through in the fine, white, vase-shaped lamps and the delicate ceramic shade for a pendant hung at just the right height.

KITCHENS

The kitchen is a functional work centre composed of fixed elements. You can plan permanent lighting in relation to the position of the work surfaces, cupboards and appliances without the need to cater for changing moods as in, say, the living room.

Kitchen lighting has been almost defined by the single fluorescent strip, but in fact this room needs much more than just one source of general light. A high level of shadow-free general lighting, important in an area where you are handling sharp knives and scalding hot pans, should always be supplemented with task lighting focused precisely where it is needed – on the sink, cooker, refrigerator and food preparation surfaces.

Colour rendering is extremely important so you can see that your ingredients are fresh. Fluorescent light has deservedly acquired a bad reputation in the past, due to poor colour rendering and a harsh appearance, but there is a pleasant alternative to positioning a fluorescent strip across the centre of the ceiling. Concealed strips on top of your wall-mounted kitchen units, fixed at the back and against the wall, transmit light upwards so it reflects back from a white-painted ceiling, creating an effective glow.

Downlights recessed into the ceiling provide pleasing pools of general light and the light sources have excellent colour-rendering properties. This solution has a significant advantage in that the luminaire is hidden and less likely to attract dirt and grease, in a room which already has a lot of equipment which needs cleaning.

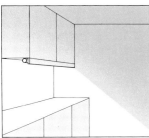

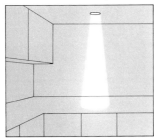

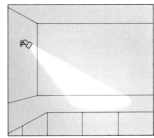

Unusual concealment for a pendant (far left) in a suspended rack surrounding the light source. Task lighting is fitted to the underside of wall units. In a streamlined white kitchen (above) ceiling downlights provide general lighting; a low pendant illuminates the adjoining dining area.

A strip light mounted underneath a cupboard and behind a baffle spreads even light on the work surface below.

A downlight placed to shed light exactly where it is needed is in itself a neat and unobtrusive source.

An adjustable spotlight mounted on the wall is a covenient and flexible source of task lighting.

The fixed elements in the kitchen allow a minimum of flexibility. Ceiling downlights throw a warm pool of light on the dining bar of this compact kitchen/diner (below).

Task lighting can add warmth to an otherwise coolly efficient kitchen, as in the sunny glow of these strip lights (right) baffle-mounted under the shelving.

Fitting a downlight

Fully recessing a downlight into a ceiling is not a very difficult job, but it does need care. Always follow any instructions supplied with the light to the letter, and if you are at all unsure on any point, particularly when it comes to providing the power supply and making the electrical connections, call in a qualified electrician – it's safer!

1. Mark out the hole for the downlight as accurately as possible on the ceiling – a template is often supplied with the light to make this easier.

2. Check that the required hole will not be interrupted by any ceiling joists, then cut it out using a padsaw. Make good the edges of the hole with filler.

3. Turn off the power at the mains, and connect the downlight up to the cable supplying it with power according to the instructions.

Supplementary lighting

There are various possibilities for task lighting, adaptable according to the amount of space in the room as a whole and the particular arrangement of appliances and storage units. You can utilize the underside of a wall-mounted kitchen unit, illuminating the gap between unit and work surface, by recessing downlights into the bottom of the cupboard. Alternatively, place fluorescent strips around the rim of the underside, concealed by a baffle. Flexible spotlights on wall- or ceiling-mounted track can be directed towards the areas where particular chores are carried out. Adjustable-arm desk lights – wall-mounted, clipped to the edge of the kitchen table, or freestanding on their own base – provide clear directional light, but make sure the fitting will not prove an obstacle as you move around between work areas.

The kichen may also double as a dining area, in which case you may want to create a less functional, more relaxed environment. Do this by judicious use of accent light, using track-mounted spotlights; gleaming kitchen utensils on metal grids are a good target. If you have concealed strips mounted above the units, position attractive glass jars and bottles along the top of the units, so they are lit from behind to create a decorative sparkle.

A combination including more than one type of light source gives the kitchen environment a varied, less monochromatic quality. You may also do much more than just prepare food in the kitchen – read, sew, or work on domestic administration, for example – so arrange suitable lighting for all these tasks. But remember that the kitchen is already cluttered with appliances: plan to create the best effect without the need for a lot of prominent hardware.

Some of the most stylish solutions have been achieved with industrial luminaires – fittings normally found in shops and offices. These often go well in the kitchen because of the predominance of laminates and metalware in the setting. So look beyond the normal home decor retail outlets for your kitchen lighting – the wider range of products for commercial interiors may well provide you with the fittings you want without spoiling the aesthetics of the room.

4. Ease the downlight into its hole, making sure it fits snugly against the ceiling surface, and fix in place – the method used depends on the light's design.

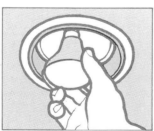

5. Double check that all is secure before fitting the lamp and restoring the power. Check that the light and its switching work correctly.

BEDROOMS

Ease and comfort are all-important in the bedroom and well-placed task lighting meets a variety of needs. Concealed lighting inside a cupboard (below left) reveals its contents clearly. Adjustable fittings wall-mounted above the bed (below) provide versatility. The more conventional bedside lamp (right) gives a pleasant, intimate glow.

Like the living room, the bedroom is an intimate setting for much varied activity: reading, relaxing, rummaging in cupboards, sleeping, dressing and working. A high level of general light should be supplemented by task lighting relevant to your bedroom-based pastimes – typing or playing a musical instrument, for instance – plus mood lighting capable of being dimmed and varied in keeping with pursuits of a more romantic nature.

A pendant luminaire is not ideal for distribution of general bedroom lighting. Stand between this light source and a drawn curtain or blind and your silhouetted naked form will unwittingly provide a shadow play for the neighbours. Much better solutions are recessed downlights or dimmer-controlled wall lights. These should provide a good level of visibility: when you're dressing, for example, you need light that will show up the torn hem of a dress or soup stains on your jacket.

Bedside lighting

Much innovation has gone into lighting controls at the bedhead, so make sure that you can switch off all bedroom lights without getting out of bed. Plan bedside lights so that either you or your partner can read on while the other sleeps. For that reason, a single tungsten strip behind a bedhead baffle is not such a good idea, even if it casts a pleasing glow on both partners. Provide individual control with two wall-mounted spotlights, one on each side of the bed, each with its own on-off switch. But spotlighting also has a drawback: it creates a rather severe contrast between the beam of light and the dark surroundings and, coming from one side, it dictates your position if you want clear, even light on your reading matter.

A good solution is a freestanding adjustable-arm luminaire with sturdy base and stem, placed on the bedside table with the bulb pointing at the wall. Less severe indirect light will

bounce down on to your bedtime book without disturbing your partner. An equally good solution is to use two translucent globe table lights, which give off a gentle omni-directional glow.

If you can wall-mount your bedside reading light, you create more space on your bedside table for books, the radio alarm clock and so on. An adjustable-arm fitting or globe light can be clamped to the wall. Another space-saving device is lighting strips built directly into the bedhead. This is a good idea in principle, but many of the marketed designs have been rather vulgar in taste. If you can't find one you like, consider customizing a more appealing design.

Storage lighting

A proportion of your bedroom space will be given over to storing your clothes and other possessions, and you'll spend a fair amount of time nosing into wardrobes and drawers. Fix a tungsten or fluorescent strip inside the wardrobe, protect it behind a baffle board and connect it up so that, operated by a pressure switch, it comes on automatically when you open the door.

If your storage cupboard is too small or awkwardly made to house internal lighting, position a couple of spotlights on a small piece of track mounted on an adjacent wall. Arrange them to shine directly into the cupboard from an angle when the door is open. If you also use spots to create task lights for dressing in front of a full-length mirror, always direct the light towards yourself and never on to the mirror.

Your dressing table may be part of an entire wall of storage units. If so, take the opportunity to fix tungsten downlights into the underside of the unit hanging above the table, or install a tungsten strip along the lower rim. In this area you can light a mirror in the same way as in the bathroom, to give good light for dry shaving or applying make-up.

BATHROOMS

Safety

DO

- follow required safety standards to keep water and electricity well apart
- recess fittings into wall or ceiling wherever possible
- put the main switch outside the door
- fit a dimmer to give low light intensity for late-night trips to the bathroom
- install a small light in the bathroom cabinet where razor blades, medicines, etc are housed

DON'T

- install hanging or adjustable fittings which you may touch or splash with water accidentally
- arrange lighting in a way that causes glaring reflections off shiny surfaces
- install conventional switches, sockets or loose flexes

Once bathrooms were regarded as stark, white and utilitarian. Today their decor is being given unprecedented attention, to make them much more comfortable and appealing. With this more luxurious concept, bathroom lighting is a design element which it is difficult to get right. Not only does the abundance of shiny reflective surfaces increase the potential for glare, but electrical safety regulations impose necessary restrictions. Electricity and water must be kept well away from each other.

Therefore a hanging central pendant, which you might brush with a wet arm as you get out of the bath, is inappropriate. So too are spotlights – it is far too tempting to adjust them by hand. The most suitable fittings are double insulated with not only all metal parts covered, but the bulb completely covered, too. A splash of cold water on a hot tungsten bulb, for example, may shatter it. Ceiling lights in the form of fixed bowls or recessed downlights are an ideal solution, achieving a high level of light that dispels early-morning miseries.

In the bathroom, it is important not to delude yourself with soft, flattering mood lighting. On the other hand, too stark and bright a light will create an unbearably pallid and ghastly effect. Light distribution, colour rendering and colour temperature are all very important, to achieve a balance that shows you to yourself in a true light that isn't too harsh – of itself and on you.

Arrange dimmer switches outside your bathroom so that you can pop in for a glass of water in the night without exposing your eyes to the full intensity of light. String-pull cords, a standard item in many bathrooms, are not attractive and can be made obsolete simply by positioning all main switches outside the bathroom.

Shower lighting

When you draw the shower curtain, make sure that it doesn't block the main source of light, leaving you to shower in gloom. Try to avoid fixing a special shower light by clever placing of the ceiling lights; but if you must light the shower itself, then a waterproof outdoor bulkhead fitting is the safest solution. Ask your supplier for advice.

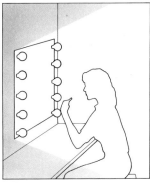

Bare bulbs mounted around three sides of a mirror are not intended merely to evoke the atmosphere of a theatre dressing room – they actually provide a very efficient spread of clear but not harsh light (above) for tasks such as shaving or applying make-up. In a confined space (top) the effect is also warming and decorative.

Well-planned distribution of light and good colour rendering create an impression of even, natural light in this spacious bathroom (left). The lights are recessed for safety's sake. A shower light concealed behind a baffle (below) accents the decorative pattern of the tiles.

Mirror lighting

Adopt the actor's style: all theatre dressing rooms have a row of bare bulbs around the edge of the mirror. Despite the glamorous image, the effect is purely functional – light shining on your face from above, below and either side of the mirror makes shaving or applying make-up much easier. A simple strip light above the mirror is a standard fitting, but it creates ridges of shadow below the nose and mouth.

As in bedroom storage, put concealed strip lighting inside bathroom cupboards – you won't want to grope in the dark for a medicine bottle or open razor. If you fit adjustable eyeball downlights in the ceiling, you can introduce an element of accent lighting – highlighting ornate taps, sparkling bottles of bath oil, wall-hanging baskets of plants or any other decorative feature. There's plenty of opportunity to create an attractive, relaxing atmosphere. You can even obtain coloured ceramic luminaires, to coordinate with sanitary-ware and bathroom furnishings.

CHILDREN'S ROOMS

An economical plug light provides a reassuring night-time glow. Designs like this box of toys (below right) should be placed out of harm's way.

Luminaires used in children's rooms should be bright, colourful and, above all, safe. The young have a fearless curiosity and disregard for the dangers of electricity and will interfere with clip-on spotlights and low-hanging pendants within range.

Provide lighting that is extra-safe, sturdy and firmly fixed to wall or ceiling – recessed downlights, wall or ceiling bowls. Freestanding uplighters and table lamps will get knocked over. Don't bother with a freestanding desk light until the child is of school age and involved with homework or hobbies. Be sure to install child-proof safety sockets, to avoid electrical accidents caused by children prodding sockets with knives, pens or fingers.

Young children spend a lot of time playing on the floor so the nursery or bedroom should be broadly and very brightly lit. Sophisticated mood lighting is, anyway, inappropriate.

Safety

DO
- provide a high level of general lighting for children playing on the floor
- fit child-proof safety sockets into walls
- equip light fittings with safety plugs carrying partly sheathed pins
- choose luminaires which are robust and can be firmly fixed to wall or ceiling

DON'T
- install portable, adjustable or fragile luminaires

Later, when the child is older and growing fast, a ceiling-mounted track of spots will provide versatile light for the inevitable parade of pastimes and hobbies, some if not all of which will be swiftly abandoned.

Considerable debate rages over light fittings that engage a child's imagination: drum lights, toy-bag lights or illuminated crescent moons, for instance. One school of thought suggests that such designs simply encourage young children to meddle with dangerous electrical equipment, but there can be no objection to these eye-catching oddities provided the child cannot reach or touch them.

Many young (and not so young) children are scared of the dark. There are plenty of reassuring nightlights on the market, but a better solution is simply to install a dimmer switch for the main light.

For older children, adjustable-arm fittings, shelf-mounted to save space (left) or free-standing (above), make attractive and versatile lighting.

WORKROOMS

Task lighting is an important feature in any type of workroom. Both the light sources and styles of luminaires should be chosen to suit the specific function of the room.

The home office

Whether you are writing a novel, running a mail order business, or simply totting up domestic bills, your home office should have a distinct identity, created by lighting which separates that space from the rest of the house. The enclosure of your desk within a tight ring of light, for instance, will aid concentration and creative thought. So underplay the general surroundings in your office or study. Use ceiling-mounted wall washers to brush bookcases and filing cabinets with gentle light, or deploy discreet uplighters to give an indirect glow.

Desk lighting

Concentrate your task light on the desk and invest in a quality luminaire. The designers' favourite is the adjustable-arm desk lamp, whether strictly functional or a complex piece of industrial sculpture, as exemplified in recent Italian designs. It is the more useful if the head swivels independently.

When seated at the desk, place the luminaire not directly in front of you but on a far corner of the desk so that light shines diagonally across your papers. Position the fitting where you can't see the glare of the bulb. Be careful in the initial choice of your light source: tungsten and linear mini-fluorescent bulbs provide soft but effective task lighting.

Visual display screens

If you work at home with a computer terminal and visual display screen, you can avoid constant headaches caused by glare, screen reflections and extremes of contrast. Block out sunlight effectively with thick curtains or blinds and use uplighters to provide soft, general and indirect artificial light. It is possible to buy task lights specially designed for computer screens. Good colour rendering and lack of flicker are the important factors here.

Whether you work with a traditional sewing machine or advanced computer terminal, task lighting should aim a tight ring of light on the work area to assist concentration.

A desk light on a flexible arm mounted above the study area (right) distributes light exactly as it is needed, lowered to direct a focused beam or raised to provide a generous pool of light.

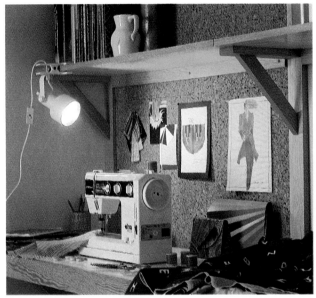

Utility rooms

Utility rooms – attic, storage room, basement, garage and workshop – require lighting that is functional, long-lasting and energy efficient rather than decorative, versatile and mood-inducing. The time you spend in such areas is put to a specific purpose and you certainly won't be entertaining guests in a utility room, so dimming, flexibility and colour appearance are not paramount considerations.

However, you must provide a good general level of visibility and, in the case of a storage basement or attic, delineate corners and steps clearly with information lighting.

Fluorescent strip on the ceiling and mini-fluorescent fittings on walls are a good option. Sturdy industrial fixtures commonly used in factories and shops are equally useful for large domestic utility areas. Once again, explore lighting outlets beyond the general run of home decor retailers. Deep bowl pendant fittings, known as hi-bays and lo-bays in the trade, are heavy and visually obtrusive but provide powerful lighting for a giant garage or storage area. Wall bulkheads are ideal for garages; they give enough light to get under the car bonnet.

Lighting a workbench

When your work involves use of industrial tools, poor lighting can result in accidents. Take care to avoid shadows, or a general light level which is gloomy or glaring. Ceiling mount a fluorescent strip directly above or just behind where you stand so that a bright, even, patternless light spills down on to the bench from both sides of you.

For industrial handywork in which colour rendering is very important – making jewellery, for example – supplement general lighting from the fluorescent strip with tungsten light from an adjustable-arm luminaire. Clip it to the corner of the workbench or let it stand on the surface on a firm base, in a position where it will not be affected by vibration or knocked over as you move and handle the necessary equipment.

ONE-ROOM LIVING

Nothing will task your ingenuity as a lighting designer more than one-room living – whether your home is an open plan area of palatial proportions or a tiny bedsit. If you cook, eat, sleep, work, wash, dress and entertain in one space, lighting design becomes the governing factor in defining inner spaces, lighting a variety of tasks, and creating a series of moods.

Flexibility should therefore be the keynote: use light fittings that are mobile – freestanding uplighters, desk lights, table lamps and standard lamps – to vary the light configurations.

Avoid at all costs a high level of general light from a central pendant, because this will reveal the mechanism of a sofabed and flood the semi-concealed kitchenette with indiscriminate illumination. You want to achieve the opposite – a sense of spatial ambiguity. When one specific area is lit, for example the dining table, the rest of your home, from the refrigerator to the clothes rack, should recede discreetly into shadow.

A rise-and-fall tungsten pendant over the dining table and a series of spotlights fixed to wall- and ceiling-mounted track will enable you to cater for different moods, especially if you put all the lights on dimmers. Freestanding, adjustable desk lights will provide task light when needed, as on the work surface or bedside table. Mount strip lighting over the cooker; position bare tungsten bulbs around the sink mirror.

Above all, be prepared to install far more light fittings in your open plan space than you would in a room of comparable size which adjoins other rooms. You have far more tasks and moods to cater for in one-room living.

If your bedsit is on the small side, don't fill it up with heavy-looking luminaires. Clip spots to bookshelves or, better still, install baffle-protected accent lighting behind the bookcase.

Several portable light fittings in one small area may cause a proliferation of untidy wires. Route them carefully along the walls, behind the furniture and under carpets where possible. If you have a platform bed raised from the floor on a scaffolding structure, clip wiring to the main structure; don't allow the flex to trail freely from an electric alarm clock and bedside light placed on a high shelf. Be careful not to overload the sockets with too many electrical appliances.

Putting up power track

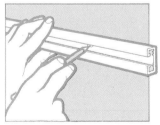

1. Hold the track in place and mark through the fixing holes on to the wall or ceiling.

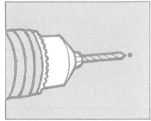

2. Drill holes at these points and insert wall plugs – cavity types on ceilings and hollow walls.

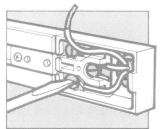

3. Feed the power cable into the track's terminal box, screw the track in place and connect up.

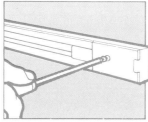

4. Check that the connections are correctly made; then screw on the terminal box cover.

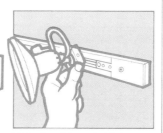

5. Finally, slide a suitable lamp on to the track, switch on and make sure everything works.

The distribution of light in one-room living can make all the difference to the sense of the overall space and the various functions it must serve. Where separate areas are defined – blinds closing off the sleeping area, shelving or tables acting as room dividers (above left) – they can also be individually lit to create localized atmospheres. Spotlights fixed to shelves, wall-mounted or freestanding (above), provide concentrated accent or task lighting and set the general light level.

OUT OF DOORS

Even at night, well-lit garden foliage lends texture and drama to a view; lighting positioned high on exterior walls highlights island beds of shrubs and makes silhouettes of hanging branches.

Just as moonlight can introduce an air of magic and mystery to your garden, so carefully applied artificial light can produce equally beautiful effects. Night lighting in your garden extends your enjoyment of its natural panorama and a little light, if it is well positioned, can have an extraordinary impact given the extreme contrasts. So your decisions about where to position light fittings out of doors and what sources to use are critical.

Outdoor lighting is complicated by the changing seasons. Lighting your garden in December will involve a different set of aesthetic criteria from those which apply in August – unless, of course, your garden is full of evergreens. Further-more, you should bear in mind the relationship between exterior and interior spaces and aim for a coherent design that harmonizes the two. A subtle, accent-lit interior will be swamped by an insensitively floodlight garden every time you draw back the curtain.

There are, however, ground rules to follow out of doors that correspond to the guidelines for interior lighting design.

- Avoid dazzle and glare by keeping the light source hidden at all times, behind a tree or stone wall, for example. Remember that a luminaire can be seen from many more angles of view on a large lawn than in a walled room.
- Use light to provide visual information for safety and comfort. If your garden has a split-level rockery, highlight the steps to prevent accidents.
- Look for objects and surfaces suitable for accent lighting – an old brick wall with creeping ivy, for example. There will be no shortage of potential: trees, shrubs and flowers, and in a large garden, perhaps, a fountain, sculpture or sundial. But don't develop a lighting scheme that spills light into neighbouring gardens – your enthusiasm for lighting may not be shared or appreciated.

Lighting trees

The texture and shape of trees and the details of blossom and foliage provide various dramatic opportunities for accent lighting. Uplight an oak tree with one or two tungsten halogen flood spots mounted on a garden wall. Use the same equip-

A bulkhead fitting placed low on the house wall is useful lighting for a pathway or patio. Neat and secure, the bulkhead is suitable also as entrance or garage lighting.

> ## Safety
>
> **DO**
> - keep main switches indoors to give you total control under all conditions
> - install *weatherproof* fittings outside and *waterproof* fittings in swimming pool, garden pond or jacuzzi
> - inspect your garden regularly to sweep leaves and debris away from light fittings
> - take professional advice on earthing, insulation and conversion to low voltage
>
> **DON'T**
> - allow flexes and fittings to interfere with chores such as lawn-mowing
> - arrange light sources at an angle which may be dazzling to visitors unfamiliar with the garden layout

ment to silhouette the branches by uplighting the wall of an adjacent building so the light is bounced back to highlight the tree. Alternatively, fix a light fitting at the centre of the tree to exude a soft glow or festoon strings of fairy lights through the branches. Local suppliers will assist in choosing fittings that are sturdy and weatherproof; screened and louvred fittings cut down glare from powerful light sources.

Lighting flowerbeds and rockeries
To accent the elegance and beauty of plantlife – the variety of shape in petals and foliage – mushroom-shaped fittings that can be spiked into the soil are extremely effective. The domes are usually made of plastic or aluminium. These fittings are movable on flexible cables so you can arrange different configurations in response to changing seasons, highlighting different groups of plants in the finest phase of their cycle.

Lighting fountains and pools
Water and light are a magical combination at night, so waste no opportunity to give your garden a shimmering allure. Accent light fountains or rock pools with wide and narrow beam spots; light on moving water – a narrow stream or fountain spray – is particularly exciting.

Install underwater light sources in the sides of a swimming pool or jaccuzzi. Have total control of the effect by putting them on a dimmer. Choose fittings that are easily removed for cleaning and maintenance, and make sure they are fully waterproof, not just weatherproof. Take advantage of water's mirror-like qualities: if a large tree is adjacent to the pool, graze it with uplight from floor-mounted baby spots.

A cohesive design
Much garden lighting is unnecessarily harsh and unpleasant – high pressure sodium lamps, for example, which muddy colours are justified on the grounds that they are security lighting meant to deter intruders. But security lighting needn't be unattractive: with a little thought, security, safety and decorative effect can be combined in one cohesive scheme. Pick fittings that will blend aesthetically with natural surroundings and make your scheme flexible: your garden is organic, constantly growing and changing.

For system installation, it is best to use a specialist contractor. If you plan to do it yourself, remember that running a power source outdoors requires extra care – all equipment must be properly insulated and earthed.

PRACTICALITIES

Having learnt about luminaires and light sources, studied the inter-linked areas of your home, and defined your requirements and those of your fellow inhabitants, you are in a position to design your artificial lighting system. Successful realization of your design depends on the power that makes it work – the distribution of electrical resources in your home, where they are and how they can be changed if existing outlets will not accommodate your requirements.

The business of installation, insulation, electrical components and accessories forms the final stage of home lighting, but don't treat these elements as last and least in the sequence. To be frank, this stage can literally be a matter of life and death. Thousands of accidents are caused in the home each year by insufficient attention to the practical matters of plugs, fuses and wiring.

Prime causes of catastrophe include fitting luminaires with bulbs that exceed the maximum wattage stated, overloading electrical sockets with too many appliances, allowing wires and cables to trail dangerously across the floor, and failing to replace old, frayed wiring in the home. Also, amateur electricians often attempt jobs that are beyond their limited expertise. However enthusiastic you are about realizing your lighting scheme, never attempt electrical installations and alterations unless you know exactly what you are doing. If you wish to examine a fixed installation, the safest course is to switch off the mains electricity supply, not just the switch or socket relating to a particular fitting. There are some tasks that do-it-yourself enthusiasts can perform perfectly well, but if you're in any doubt at all, call in a qualified professional. Remember that to play with electricity is to play with fire.

Purchasing equipment

The first principle is that you should always buy equipment from a reputable retailer and check on the manufacturer and country of origin. With a reliable supplier you have the assurance that the fittings are well made and conform to required safety standards. Pay close attention to printed instructions and conditions of use attached to any electrical equipment.

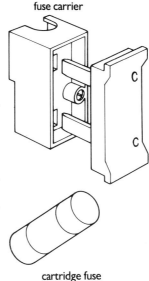

fuse carrier

cartridge fuse

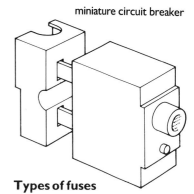

miniature circuit breaker

Types of fuses

Most fuse boxes and consumer units hold fuse carriers – those for lighting are colour coded white. Older types contain bare fuse wire: modern ones use cartridge fuses. In very modern systems, miniature circuit breakers replace fuses. To 'repair' these, push the reset button on their face.

Safety first

The mains electricity infrastructure in your home has a set of built-in safety valves – the fuses. These are designed to burn out as soon as excessive current flows in the wiring system, so cutting off the current before major damage occurs. There are two basic forms: rewireable fuses in which a short length of wire runs between two terminals and can be replaced when the fuse burns out, and cartridge fuses, requiring replacement of the whole unit after a blow-out.

When replacing a fuse, always remember to switch off the mains supply and trace the cause of the fuse blowing – that is, the point where the circuit is faulty or overloaded. If a fuse blows repeatedly, call in a qualified electrician to check out the system. Wiring is less reliable in homes more than thirty years old, so if you have bought, or propose to buy, an older property, get the wiring examined by a professional.

Safety rules

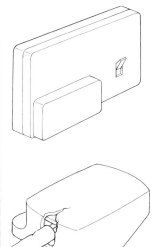

There are a number of safety tips to remember when connecting up your lighting equipment:

- Treat high voltage mains supply with respect; switch off the current at the wall socket before handling any luminaire, even when fitting a new light bulb.
- Check for worn or frayed flex, broken or burnt components. Rectify the faults immediately.
- Make sure your hands are completely dry before handling electrical equipment. An added safety precaution is to wear rubber-soled shoes or stand on a rubber mat when touching electrical fittings.
- Never touch different metal parts of a fitting with both hands in such a way that you effectively form a connection between the two parts.
- When making connections, ensure that all bared strands of wire are neatly inserted into the relevant socket or plug terminal and that there are no loose strands that may short the circuit by connecting the main wires.
- Ensure that you have the correct tools for the job — insulated screwdriver, wire trimmers, cutters, and so on.

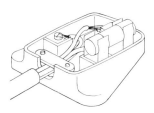

Rewiring a circuit fuse

Take the fuse carrier from the fuse box, remove the old fuse wire, and thread a new piece rated at 5 amps through the

hole in the carrier's bridge. Wind the ends around the terminal screws and tighten up carefully.

Replacing a plug fuse

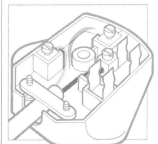 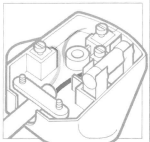

Undo the retaining screw found between the plug's prongs, and remove the back. Prise out the old cartridge

fuse. Clip a new one (normally 3 amp) in its place, and then replace the plug back and tighten the fixing screw.

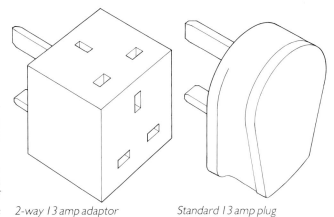

2-way 13 amp adaptor   *Standard 13 amp plug*

Watts, amps and volts

Each luminaire you buy will specify a maximum wattage for the bulb to be used – don't exceed this specification. Wattage measures the rate at which electricity is consumed and indicates the power of the light source.

Electricity is also measured in amperes (amps) and volts. Amperage is the measurement of the speed at which an electric current flows. The quicker and stronger the flow of electricity, the greater the number of amps, and the larger the wires and plugs needed to carry it. In Britain, 13 amp plugs are the standard method of connections for most domestic luminaires.

Volts measure the pressure of electricity flowing along the wire. The greater the pressure, the larger the number of volts, and the stronger the conductors must be. In Britain, the average pressure of a domestic electric circuit – known as the mains supply – is 240 volts; in the USA, it is 120 volts.

Electrical provision

An electric current consists of moving electrons that need a complete circuit on which to flow, forming a continuous chain from the mains connection to the appliance and back again. Light switches, wall-mounted or attached to the appliance, perform the function of completing or breaking the circuit, to turn the light on or off.

Every home supplied with electricity from the national grid via a nearby sub-station has an infrastructure of electrical provision – wiring, switch locations and electrical sockets – connecting your lighting equipment to the electricity supply. The path of the wiring is concealed and in the bathroom, of course, for safety reasons, switches and sockets are omitted. Often you will choose to work within the given limits of this electrical infrastructure – by plugging freestanding uplighters into available sockets, for example. You may however, have the inclination, design flair and money to have floorboards lifted and parts of the walls and ceilings cut away, to relocate wires so additional sockets and wall outlets can be provided. In this case, don't carry out plastering or decorating in the rooms until all work on electrical alterations has finished.

Plugs old and new

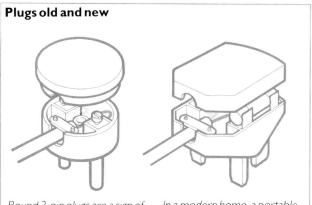

Round 2-pin plugs are a sign of old lighting circuitry that ought to be replaced.

In a modern home, a portable light plugs into a ring power circuit using a 13 amp plug.

Making the connection

The electricity in the domestic mains supply in the home is different from the electricity used, say, in a torch. In the home it is AC – Alternating Current – flowing back and forth on the circuit; in a torch battery, it is DC – Direct Current – a continuous flow of electricity in one direction. For lighting equipment connected up to an AC mains supply in the UK, the traditional method to ensure that a fitting is safe has been to provide a reliable means of connection to earth. The luminaire has an earth wire, in addition to the live and neutral wires carrying the current, which connects it to an earth terminal. In wiring a plug you must connect all three wires to

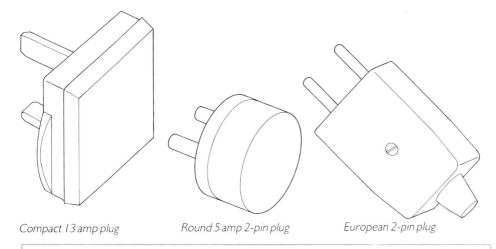

Compact 13 amp plug   *Round 5 amp 2-pin plug*   *European 2-pin plug*

The square-pin 13 amp plug is now regarded as standard for both domestic appliances and plug-in lighting, and comes in a limited choice of colours and attractive designs. Old-fashioned round 2-pin plugs (not to be confused with the European 2-pin plug) are still available, but, for safety's sake, homes with this type of socket should be rewired. Take the opportunity to add extra sockets – overloading circuits through the over-use of adaptors is also dangerous.

Wiring up a plug

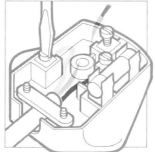
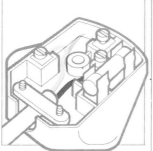

1. Remove the flex's outer sheath, cut the wires to length, then strip them of the last 6mm (¼ in) or so of insulation.

2. Secure the bare ends in the terminal blocks – brown to live (marked L); blue to neutral (N); green/yellow to earth (E).

3. Screw the flex grip hard down on to the flex sheathing. Ensure the fuse is correctly rated for the light.

the correct terminals; the earth wire is identifiable by its green and yellow insulation (European standard). Earthed fittings will usually carry a label with the warning 'This appliance must be earthed'.

There is a second type of light fitting classified by the British Standards Institution – the double-insulated fitting. This has no earth wire but only a live (brown) wire and neutral (blue) wire. This type of luminaire depends on the thickness and quality of its insulating material to ensure safety without the need for earthing. It is perfectly safe because all the components that come into contact with the electric current have at least two layers of insulation around them. The label on this

type of appliance will either state that it is double-insulated or show the international symbol of a square within a square.

When wiring up a plug you can connect the two wires of a double-insulated light fitting to the live and neutral terminals of a three-pin plug, simply ignoring the earth terminal. Always make sure that no 'whiskers' of bare wire stray outside the plug terminal.

To increase the length of flex on a luminaire, the wires can be joined by means of a connecting block with wiring terminals inside. Check carefully that you are wiring it up correctly, matching blue wire to blue, brown to brown, and the earth wires, if they exist, forming a separate connection.

Lamp choices

1. General service tungsten bulbs – for everyday use.

2-6. Decorative tungsten bulbs – in several shapes and sizes.

7. Crown-silvered bulbs – mainly for spotlights; they throw the light back on to the reflector.

8. Tungsten strip lights – an alternative to mini-fluorescents; used under shelves, etc.

9. Round bulbs – better looking than ordinary bulbs, they also give a softer light.

10-11. Reflector bulbs – focused beams for accent floodlights.

12. PAR lamps – wide or narrow beam, weatherproof lamps useful for display illumination.

13-14. Tungsten-halogen reflectors – bright floodlights for paintings, ornaments, etc.

15-16. Tungsten-halogen display lamps – for wall washers, downlights and floodlights.

17-18. Linear tungsten-halogen floodlighting lamps – for very powerful outdoor floodlighting.

19-20. Fluorescent strip lights – used for general illumination.

21. Circular fluorescent lamps – an alternative to strips.

22. U-lamps – as above.

23-26. Mini-fluorescents – for wall lights, concealed lighting. Note: The lamps shown here are of the Edison Screw (ES) type, but most also come in bayonet fitting form.

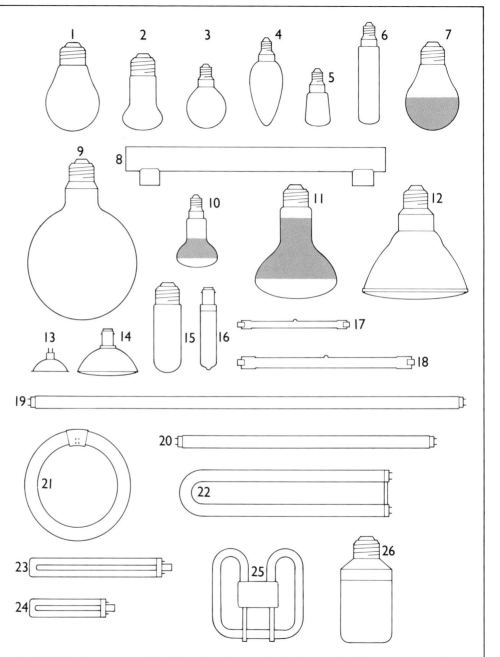

Bulbs

There is enormous variety in the bulbs developed and manufactured for domestic use. They come in all shapes and sizes, designed to perform a multitude of tasks. Tungsten filament bulbs are still the most popular, but tungsten halogen, linear fluorescent and mini-fluorescent are becoming more commonly used.

Tungsten bulbs are available with pearlized, clear or coloured glass, with silvered fronts so that light is directed downwards on to a reflector, and as internally silvered reflector lamps. They are made in a variety of shapes – standard, mushroom, candle, strip or golfball – to suit different decorative needs and to fit deep or shallow luminaires. The way these bulbs are attached to the fittings varies from country to country. In Britain there are four different bulb caps: bayonet cap, small bayonet cap, Edison screw, small Edison screw.

Household tungsten bulbs range from 25 to 150 watts; low voltage tungsten halogen from 20 to 100 watts. Linear fluorescent strips can range from 4 watts (150mm nominal length) to 125 watts (2400mm nominal length). The new generation of energy-saving compact mini-fluorescents are normally within the 7 to 25 wattage rating, but note that a 25-watt mini-fluorescent emits the same amount of light as a 100-watt tungsten bulb. Shapes of mini-fluorescents range from jam-jar style to slim linear strip. A useful device is a flat bar formed from a narrow tube doubled back on itself in a hairpin effect, which enables flush fitting against a wall.

If your choice of lighting includes neon or high pressure sodium light sources, consult a lighting professional to determine the correct bulbs to use. Overall, given the sheer diversity of the range available, it is advisable always to ask your supplier for advice on wattage ratings and shapes.

Measuring light

With your lighting equipment expertly and safely connected to the mains electricity supply in the home, you can at last see the effect of artificial light in various rooms. Simply using your own eyes, you can assess the visual comfort and impact of the light around you. For those interested in the way light is technically quantified, a lumen is a measure of the concentration of light arriving at a given surface from a given direction; lux is a measure of lumens per square metre (in imperial units, lumens per square foot are called footcandles). In a given situation, the light level can be measured with a piece of equipment called an illuminance meter. Maximum and minimum lux levels have been calculated by electrical engineers around the world for particular interiors; for example, in office areas, a level of 500 lux is suggested as suitable general lighting for clerical work.

In your home, the lighting contributes to comfort and decorative effect and functionally must match your personal requirements. Ultimately, a simple, off-the-cuff qualitative judgement of light levels will be more practical than any amount of scientific calculation.

Light levels

Technical measurements of light are largely irrelevant in the home where the main criteria should be your own judgement of what is most comfortable to the eye and conducive to the mood you want to create. But there are a number of points of comparison worth bearing in mind:

A level of 500 lux is recommended for general reading and clerical work in artificially lit interiors. But for more detailed work – on a printed text for instance – a 50 per cent increase (750 lux) is suggested.

In comparison to artificial light levels, on a cloudless sunny day, the sun gives off 100,000 lux. And even an overcast sky produces 5,000 lux of light.

The quantity of light required by a person to perform a particular task is directly related to age. At age 40 the requirement is three times that for a 10-year-old. At age 60 it is 15 times that for a 10-year-old.

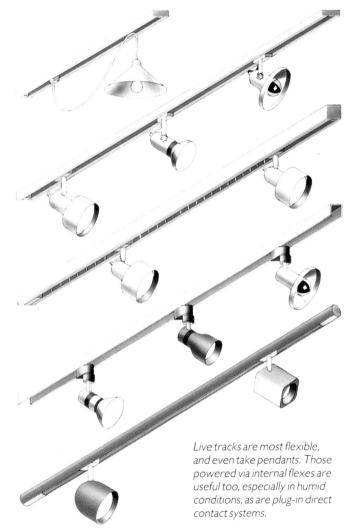

Live tracks are most flexible, and even take pendants. Those powered via internal flexes are useful too, especially in humid conditions, as are plug-in direct contact systems.

Lighting track

First developed for offices and shops, lighting track has long been an important accessory in home lighting design. Basically, a track is an elongated electric socket which enables several luminaires to be attached along its length. It can be floor-, ceiling- or wall-mounted and comes in a number of guises.

There are different kinds of track mountings serving different functions. Live track enables spotlights to be plugged in and slid into position at any point along the length of the track fitting. Fixed bar track consists of a predetermined number of spotlights mounted immovably on a bar: it lacks flexibility but has the advantage of being relatively inexpensive. There are newer forms of flexible track which offer the manoeuvrability provided by live track, although in this case the track is not completely live. These carry the power for the luminaires within a flexible cable, or provide a direct contact system with a series of snap-in sockets.

Because of variations between manufacturers' approaches, make sure that the track you buy and the luminaires you want to fix on to it are compatible. This need not mean choosing all components from a given range. Again, ask the supplier for advice.

Dimmer controls

Throughout discussion of suitable luminaires and light sources for different situations, it has been apparent that dimmers are an efficient way to create atmosphere with lower levels of light and at the same time reduce electricity costs by using less power. Dimmer controls are usually combined with an on-off switch, and installation is a relatively simple exercise.

Like luminaires, dimmers have a wattage rating and it is important that the fittings they control should not exceed the figure stated. Tungsten and mains-voltage tungsten halogen sources can be dimmed easily; mini-fluorescents cannot be dimmed at all, which puts a question mark against their desirability in a domestic environment. It is technically possible to dim linear fluorescent, neon and low-voltage tungsten halogen sources, but the process is really too costly and cumbersome to be worth the average householder's time, money and effort.

As regards the operation of dimmers, you can choose from touch-plate control, rotary or sliding action switches and foot-pedal control. A touch-plate control dimmer can be wired up to the flex of a table lamp or desk light. There are even automatic dimmers operated by electronic photo cells: light sensors detect the level of natural light outside the room and automatically adjust the artificial light level accordingly.

Time delay, sensory and computer controls

Apart from dimmers, there are a host of other controls which will adjust artificial light in our homes to make life safer, easier and more comfortable.

On the staircase in shared-entry accommodation, for example, time delay switches allow you to switch on the light and descend or ascend the staircase in brightly lit surroundings; the light switches itself off automatically a few minutes later to save on electricity bills. There are electronic audio controls linked to the lighting which will automatically switch on the lights in a room as soon as a voice or noise is heard at a given level. Another sensory device detects the presence of a living, breathing human being and switches the lights on automatically.

As microchip technology becomes cheaper and more widely utilized in the home, the computerized lighting controls that are already a feature of industrial and commercial buildings will become more popular with householders too. These controls link all the mechanical functions of the home — heating, ventilation, lighting, the movement of blinds and curtains even — to a central domestic computer. You can programme the computer by tapping out commands on a keyboard, planning exactly when and where you want lights to go on and off. This type of home automation is particularly useful for pre-programming the lighting as a security measure when you go on holiday.

Plugs, switches and cables

If you have applied light with subtlety and chosen luminaires with style, don't waste your design flair by playing safe with functional accessories lacking any visual appeal. In particular, plugs, light switches and wires don't have to be dull: you can buy them in bright colours suited to the design of your light fittings and add a little extra panache to the room. If your lighting design calls unavoidably for a long and obtrusive extension lead, pick an appropriately coloured curly cable and make a virtue of its presence.

But don't expose wires just for the sake of it: concealed cabling is usually neater and safer.

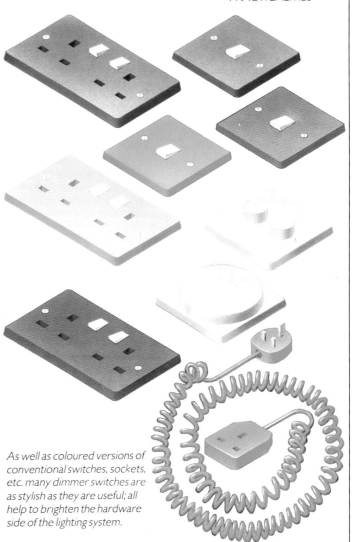

As well as coloured versions of conventional switches, sockets, etc. many dimmer switches are as stylish as they are useful; all help to brighten the hardware side of the lighting system.

Other accessories

As domestic lighting design departs from traditional configurations and explores new ideas, so the number of helpful accessories grows; for example, lamp clamps that attach light fittings to a desk top or shelving; door-frame switches that facilitate lighting in dark cupboards, activating the light every time the cupboard door swings open. There are many such details that add versatility and style to your lighting design; investigate all the possibilities before making your final choice.

MAKING YOUR OWN LIGHTS

Despite the wealth of home lighting products on the market, there will always be individual design ideas that fall outside the scope of the manufactured ranges. The option here is to make your own lights.

Innovation and stylish experiment form an integral part of good lighting design – and it only takes an added measure of application and skill to move beyond decorative grouping of coloured candles to making customized luminaires. But as a word of warning, be very careful with the wiring and fitting of plugs or connectors. Don't attempt do-it-yourself lighting unless you understand the principles of electricity.

Lamp bases have traditionally been improvised from wine bottles and ceramic vases; even from such a simple object as a brick with a hole drilled through it. Choose a material that is heat-resistant and not a conductor of electricity. Wires, plugs, bulb holders and lampshade frames can be bought as individual accessories for assembly. Lampshades can be made up from a variety of fabrics and reflective materials. Thin plastic sheets and paper (except a stiff parchment) should be used with care, as they could be a fire risk.

Fabric lampshades offer good opportunities for stylish colour accessorizing, but they also call for nimble fingers and proven needlework skills. The simplest lampshade to make is a handkerchief shade – a draped effect from a square of fabric with a hole cut in the centre, fitted over a standard utility ring frame. A Tiffany shade requires a frame of precisely the right shape and a more elaborate process of construction to tailor fabric to the shape, but it can also be fitted with a simple, gathered cover. There are coolie and drum shapes which require the appropriate frames for a successful result, but they are relatively easy to sew.

One advantage of making your own lights is the ability to renovate and put back into service old, classic lamp bases. Provide new shades and design individual, decorative patterns, using such techniques as batik, stencilling and embroidery. To complement rather than replace manufactured lighting products, your own custom lights can be fun – whether you make them for pleasure or for reasons of economy.

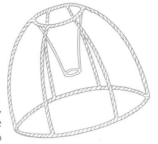
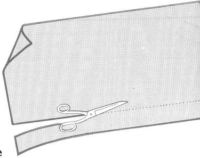

Simple fabric lampshade
Protect the metal frame from rust by winding cotton tape over all struts. For simple gathered shades paint with gloss instead.

Measure round the bottom ring for width of fabric, adding 30mm (1½ in) for seam. Add 130mm (5 in) to depth of frame for fabric length, for hems.

Making a lamp base

Any lightweight base or tall shape needs weighting with pebbles or sand to make it safe for use.

Lamp fitments are available with adjustable flanges so that they can be wedged into a narrow bottle or jar neck.

A wider-necked jar should be first plugged with a cork disc, which should fit snugly inside. Cut the hole for the lamp fitment carefully.

After weighting the lamp base, insert the cork and use glue or sticky tape to help wedge it in, and then put in the lamp fitment.

Folding fabric right side facing inwards, machine stitch down edge, then press seam allowances flat. For fraying fabrics, make a French seam.

Fold over twice to make a 10mm (½ in) hem round both the top and bottom edges of the fabric. Stitch, leaving a small gap for threading elastic.

Use a safety pin to thread two lengths of elastic through the hems; each piece slightly shorter than the circumferences of the shade. Stitch ends.

Turn the cover right side out and pull over the frame. The bottom area fits fairly tightly. Align the seam behind a strut, then arrange gathers evenly.

Paper lampshade

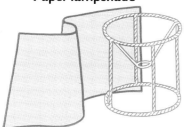

Tape the metal frame as before; painting will not do as the shade is stitched to the tape. Cut rectangle of paper to fit frame plus 10mm (½ in) overlaps.

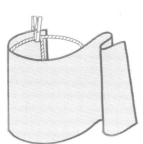

Use all-purpose fabric or paper glue to position cylinder round frame. Fabric can be ironed on to stiff bonding paper for a shade to match curtains.

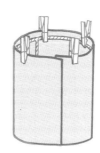

Position and glue join behind one of the vertical struts. Clothes pegs anchor the paper cover while the glue sets. Trim overlap close to struts.

For extra firmness, stitch the shade to the frame round top and bottom ring, then trim overlap. Glue a decorative braid over the stitching, or leave plain.

Pleated paper lampshade

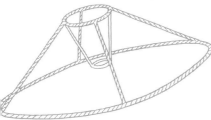

A coolie shape for a pleated shade can be taped or painted as the stitching winds round the rings. The central one need not be taped.

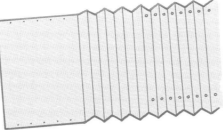

Measure base ring and double this length for paper width. Allow 40mm (1 ½ in) for overlap at the top and bottom of the shade.

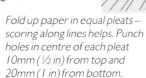

Fold up paper in equal pleats – scoring along lines helps. Punch holes in centre of each pleat 10mm (½ in) from top and 20mm (1 in) from bottom.

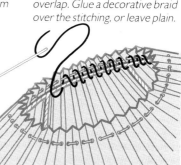

Glue pleat overlap and position behind one vertical strut. Thread cord through holes to fit top and bottom rings, and sew over this to hold shade to rings.

INDEX

Acknowledgments

Consultant: André Tammes of the Lighting Design
Partnership, Edinburgh

The author would like to thank: John Phillips of Habitat; James
Russell and J. F. Caminada of Philips Lighting, Eindhoven,
Netherlands; Janet Turner of Concord Lighting, London;
Wendy Smith; Brendan Thorpe; Madame Gibeaux of Lita
Lighting, Orleans, France

Illustrators: Graham Corbet; Terry Evans; Richard Phipps; Ed
Stewart

Picture credits:
Abbreviations: CO – Conran Octopus Ltd; EWA – Elizabeth
Whiting & Associates; *MMC – La Maison de Marie Claire;
WOI – The World of Interiors*

Abitare/Gabriele Basilico 60-1; Arcaid/Richard Bryant
(architects: Thomas Brent Associates) 6-7; Guy Bouchet 66;
Michael Boys 42, 43; Camera Press 21, 30-1, 36 above, 50, 52,
53, 56 right, 63, 64-5; CO 26; CO/Simon Brown (architect:
Shay Cleary) 8-9, 9, 16-17, 54-5; CO/Simon Brown 48 (both),
60 centre; CO/John Heseltine 19; CO/Ken Kirkwood
(designer: George Powers) 45; CO/Peter Mackertich 59 left;
Conran's 49, 61; EWA 58; EWA/Richard Davies 34-5; EWA/
Michael Dunne 24-5; EWA/Neil Lorimer 31; Susan Griggs
Agency/Michael Boys 26-7, 59 right; Habitat 22-3, 23 (both),
25 below, 29, 36 below, 39, 51, 57, 62 (both), 65, 67; Ken
Kirkwood 25 above, 38-9; Light Limited 32-3; *MMC*/Gilles de
Chabaneix 37; *MMC*/Yves Duronsoy 40-1; *MMC*/Pierre
Hussenot 17, 41; *MMC*/Serge Korniloff 54; *Maison Française*/
Christian Gervais 11; Mothercare UK Ltd 60 left; Doug
Tomlinson 8; *WOI*/Michael Boys 44, 46, 46-7; *WOI*/Fritz von
der Schulenburg 56 left